Pupils with Severe Learning Disabilities who Present Challenging Behaviours

A WHOLE SCHOOL APPROACH TO ASSESSMENT AND INTERVENTION

by

John Harris
Margaret Cook
Graham Upton

British Library Cataloguing in Publication Data

A CIP catalogue record for this book is available from the British Library

ISBN 1 873791 86 0
First published 1996

BILD Publications is the publishing office of the
British Institute of Learning Disabilities
(Registered Charity No. 1019663)

Published and distributed by
bild
Wolverhampton Road, Kidderminster
Worcestershire DY10 3PP
Telephone: 01562 850251

Printed and bound by
The Cookley Printers Limited
56 Bridge Road, Cookley, Kidderminster, Worcs., England DY10 3SB

CONTENTS

Acknowledgements

The authors and the British Institute of Learning Disabilities gratefully acknowledge the support of the Mental Health Foundation both for a research project grant and additional funding to assist publication of this book. We should like to thank the staff and pupils of nine special schools who participated in this research; the members of our research steering group (Peter Mittler, John Corbett, Christina Tilstone, Rob Ashdown, Beryl Smith and Justin Russell); Malcolm Jones and Phillipa Russell who read our research report and made a number of helpful suggestions on how this could be made more accessible to a wider audience. We are grateful to Grace Simmonds who typed the manuscript and to Philip Tilstone whose editorial skills enhanced the final stages of production.

The table on page 26 is printed with permission of Cambridge University Press.

Chapter 1

CHALLENGING BEHAVIOUR IN AN EDUCATIONAL CONTEXT

Introduction

This book is about a small number of children who make exceptional demands upon their parents, carers and teachers. These demands arise from a combination of severe learning disabilities and challenging behaviours. For a child with a severe learning disability, developmental and educational progress is likely to be slow and heavily dependent upon intensive support from family and professionals. For some children, the area of development most affected is the ability to organise their own behaviour in ways which are both intelligible and acceptable to other people. When parents and professionals fail to make sense of a child's behaviour, they are likely to be disturbed and concerned. When that same behaviour is dangerous or socially unacceptable, it is likely to be placed centre stage as the main focus for parental attention and professional interest.

For pupils with severe learning disabilities, problem behaviour presents a challenge in many different ways, depending upon the setting and those who are in the child's company. At school, the most obvious and damaging consequence of challenging behaviour is that it undermines the provision of appropriate developmental and educational experiences. Thus behaviour, which occurs initially either directly or indirectly as a consequence of a learning disability, often becomes a major obstacle to further learning and development. In the absence of effective intervention to break into this cycle, challenging behaviour is likely to lead to inappropriate or

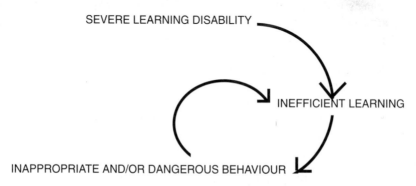

SEVERE LEARNING DISABILITY

INEFFICIENT LEARNING

INAPPROPRIATE AND/OR DANGEROUS BEHAVIOUR

inadequate learning experiences which, in turn, are followed by ever increasing levels of challenging behaviour.

At this point an example of the complex interrelationship between learning and challenging behaviour may be helpful.

Charles is a tall muscular 17 year old who attends a school for pupils with severe learning disabilities. During the morning he had refused to board the school bus and had become violent and aggressive when encouraged to do so:

1.00 p.m. In the outside play area, Charles is hot and distressed. After the lunch break he refuses to go back into the FE unit. He begins to grab and kick at the female deputy head who has been trying to persuade him to go inside. When he knocks her glasses off, the head comes out and attempts to calm Charles by holding his hands and speaking quietly to him. When they both try physically to guide Charles into the building, he resists by sitting on the ground and shouts out, 'Calm down. Not in the Unit'. The head and his deputy stay with Charles and try to offer reassurance by holding him while he is on the ground. Three attempts to persuade Charles to return to the building are met with physical resistance, verbal aggression and Charles sitting down.

1.20 p.m. The head and deputy decide to try and help Charles improve his self control before asking him to move back into the FE unit. They allow him to stay seated. The head sits behind Charles with his arms around him while the deputy sits across his legs to prevent him kicking. They say, 'Let us help you Charles. Say, "Please help me" Charles. No kicking'. Charles cries and shouts. The head says, 'If you want to cry, you cry, but you're just making a noise to block us out'. The deputy says 'Don't block us out. We want to help you. We're going to stay here with you'. Charles struggles, shouts and spits.

1.40 p.m. Still holding Charles on the floor. The head says, 'When you feel you are going to hurt someone, you must say "Help me please" and let them hold your hands'. Charles shouts, 'No hold hands', and screams. The head and deputy continue trying to teach Charles the 'Help me please' routine.

1.50 p.m. Charles is calm. The deputy repeats the 'Help me please' routine and Charles offers his hands to be held.

1.55 p.m. The deputy says, 'What did Mr. Brown say?' Charles answers, 'Help me please'.

2.00 p.m. With verbal encouragement Charles gets up and joins his class group which by this time has moved out of the FE unit into the garden.

2.10 p.m. While still being supervised by the head teacher, Charles hits a member of staff in the back and immediately says, 'Say sorry'. This is repeated before

Charles is restrained by the head. When he is released he hits the member of staff again. The head holds both his hands and takes Charles through the 'Help me please' routine and then lets go. As soon as he is let go, he hits the member of staff again and says, 'Say sorry'. When this is repeated, the head and deputy hold Charles and move him, struggling, into a classroom. They both hold him, the head from behind and deputy in front while they go through the 'Help me please' routine. The head says, 'You hit Lili'. Charles says, 'Hit Lili'. The head says, 'You should have said "Help me please" then I would have come and held your hands'.

2.20 p.m. Charles is quieter. The deputy says, 'You control yourself; put your arms down gently'. Charles obeys. The head and deputy let go of Charles. The head says' 'Are you controlled?'. Charles says, 'Yes'. The head and Charles go out to the garden where Charles agrees to pick up rubbish and place it in a bag.

This example illustrates the complexity of working with pupils with severe learning difficulties who present problem behaviours. First, there is an obvious difficulty for the staff in understanding why the non-compliant and aggressive behaviours occur. Charles' behaviour does not appear to be motivated by an attempt to test the rules or to rebel against authority figures. He seems to be apprehensive about joining his teaching group, but there is no obvious reason for this. Similarly, it is difficult to see why he hits the member of staff; she hadn't reprimanded him or upset him in any other way and Charles didn't express pleasure or remorse; on the contrary, the phrase 'Say sorry' sounds more like an attempt to anticipate what another adult is likely to say in response to his hitting. On the surface, it is difficult to explain Charles' behaviour in terms of the thoughts and feelings which we usually use to interpret our own behaviour and the behaviour which we encounter when dealing with other people.

Secondly, in the context of the school, the behaviours are problematic for a number of reasons:

- They reduce Charles' opportunities for learning: he is in the playground instead of being in the classroom with his peers.

- When Charles becomes aggressive in the classroom, his behaviour disrupts the activities of all those in his teaching group.

- There is the risk of injury, especially to staff who are trying to help him, but also to other pupils who are nearby.

- When he is being aggressive, staff try to keep Charles away from other pupils; his behaviour therefore leads to social isolation.

- His behaviour prevented a trip in the school bus; it is unlikely that staff will wish to take Charles out of school into the community if there is a risk that he will be aggressive or non-compliant.

- Two senior staff have spent a considerable amount of time with Charles, simply trying to persuade him to join his teaching group.

- The fact that Charles is occasionally aggressive and stubbornly non-compliant is likely to reduce the options for post school provision.

For Charles, it seems that non-compliance and aggression constitute a significant barrier to learning and prevent him from participating in a wide range of sound and educational activities.

Thirdly, while the staff have shown great patience, they have not been particularly successful in responding to the behaviour. The episode lasted nearly one and a half hours and for much of that time Charles was being physically restrained. For part of the time another member of staff was being hit. At the end of the episode, it is not clear why Charles settled down and rejoined his group. One might also speculate on whether the staff have learned from this incident about the best ways of responding to Charles when he is violent or when he refuses to participate in teaching activities.

Challenging behaviour
The term 'challenging behaviour' has become, in recent years, widely accepted as the most appropriate term to describe the behaviour presented by Charles and other children and adults with learning disabilities and, in this book, we have generally used it in preference to other descriptions such as 'problem behaviour' or 'inappropriate behaviour'. As a description of a range of highly varied behaviours which have the common feature of posing social, developmental and educational problems, 'challenging behaviour' has a number of advantages and, also, some significant disadvantages.

The advantages associated with the term 'challenging behaviour' are more concerned with the implicit messages which it is intended to convey rather than definitional precision. Essentially, there are three important presuppositions associated with the term 'challenging'.

First, a challenge is not a personal feature carried around by individuals; instead, a challenge expresses the idea of a relationship between one person or group of people and another person or group of persons. Challenging behaviour is not a characteristic of the person in the same way that heart disease or a broken leg personally belongs to the person. Challenging behaviour represents a relationship between

4

the behaviour displayed by one person, or persons, and the interpretation placed on that behaviour by other people. Both parties in this relationship, therefore, contribute to the challenge and both share the responsibility for addressing or overcoming it.

Secondly, the interpretation placed on behaviour is sensitive to contextual features such as the age of the person presenting the behaviour, the setting where the behaviours occur and the relative status of the people concerned. While it may be acceptable for a toddler to throw an empty cup on the floor because it is empty, this would not be regarded as appropriate behaviour by an adult in a restaurant.

Thirdly, behaviours are not identified as 'challenging' in themselves; rather it is their outcomes or consequences which determine whether they are seen as challenging or not. Whether outcomes of behaviour are judged as beneficial or detrimental is influenced by the values of those who make the judgment. In the case of Charles, loss of educational opportunity, isolation from peers, risk of injury, etc. are all seen as negative outcomes because of the high value we place on education, social inter-action and safety. Thus, many different behaviours may all be grouped under the heading 'challenging'; at the same time, some behaviours which are clearly very challenging in one setting are neither challenging nor in any way problematic in another. For example, children are encouraged to run around during recreation periods, but they are expected to sit quietly during lessons.

The main problem with the term 'challenging behaviour' is the difficulty in developing a precise definition from a relational description. This difficulty is discussed in more detail below. However, it is worth noting that, whereas the term 'challenging behaviour' has probably helped many professionals and carers to develop a better understanding of why some behaviours are problematic and to think more positively about intervention strategies, there is still considerable confusion about what exactly counts as a 'challenge'. Indeed, critics would argue that reliance on a 'definition' derived from the meaning professionals and carers assign to behaviour, precludes the establishment of any reliable diagnostic criteria.

For example, consider the case of Mary, a child with autism and many bizarre and inappropriate behaviours. Occasionally, Mary takes all her clothes off and engages in sexually explicit behaviour. When this happens in Miss Brown's class, she takes no notice of Mary but fills the sink with water and foam bath oil. Water play is Mary's favourite activity. Miss Brown then tells Mary, in a matter of fact way, that she can only play with the water if she has all her clothes on. Within a few minutes Mary is dressed and happily exploring the characteristics of floating materials at the sink. When the same thing happens in Mr. Smith's class, he immediately becomes embarrassed and anxious about how he should respond to Mary. He feels unable to approach her but he finds it impossible to ignore her. Eventually, he asks for help from the head teacher and they decide that Mary has challenging behaviour.

When they discuss Mary's behaviour with Miss Brown, she agrees that Mary takes her clothes off but denies that this represents 'challenging behaviour'.

The obvious explanation is that the relationship between Miss Brown and Mary's behaviour is not problematic, whereas the relationship between Mr. Smith and the same behaviour leads to anxiety, uncertainty and classroom disruption. The distinction between behaviour which is and is not perceived as challenging lies in the personal and professional resources of the two teachers who are with Mary when she takes her clothes off. There is agreement insofar as they both disapprove of nudity and overt sexual behaviour in the classroom, but the two teachers disagree as to whether this behaviour presents them with a 'challenge'.

Challenging behaviour in schools

In schools for pupils with severe learning difficulties, there is increasing concern among staff about the challenge presented by pupils with aggressive or socially inappropriate behaviour. The mounting interest in pupils who present challenging behaviour is associated with a number of changes in the care and education of children and adults with learning disabilities.

1. Care in the Community for adults with learning disabilities has resulted in the closure of many long stay 'mental handicap hospitals' and the expectation that most pupils leaving school will find accommodation and undertake daytime activities in ordinary community settings. Whereas, in the past, young people who presented severe challenges would have been admitted to long term residential accommodation, this is no longer regarded as the most favourable option.

2. The closure programme for the old hospitals has forced health and social services to resettle adults with challenging behaviour who were previously 'contained' in long stay hospitals. The challenge of supporting people with challenging behaviours in ordinary homes has prompted a number of influential publications and conferences. Most recent among the publications from the Department of Health is the report of the Project Group chaired by Professor Jim Mansell (1993). The debate about community based provision for adults has, in turn, increased the awareness of professionals and carers responsible for children with challenging behaviour. For example, in response to the interest stimulated by the Mansell Report, the Mental Health Foundation established a committee to inquire into services for children and young people with learning disabilities who present challenging behaviours.

3. Following the establishment of a committee of inquiry under the chairmanship of Lord Elton into the behaviour of pupils in ordinary schools, in 1989 the government published a report entitled *Discipline in Schools*. More recently, the Department for Education has circulated official guidelines on Pupil

Behaviour and Discipline (Department of Education, 1994). While neither of these initiatives, is directly concerned with pupils with severe learning disabilities, both have helped to focus attention on standards of behaviour for all pupils.

4. The introduction of the National Curriculum in schools for pupils with severe learning difficulties has emphasised the importance of formal education. At the same time, increased attention to assessment and record keeping has helped to pinpoint pupils who, because of their behaviour, are difficult to engage in curriculum based activities relevant to their age and ability. Inspection of special schools under OFSTED provides another mechanism for the identification of pupils who are unable to participate in classroom activities because of their behaviour. The difficulties experienced by SLD schools in making appropriate provision for pupils with challenging behaviour were noted by HMI in their 1994 report to Department for Education (Tobin, 1994).

5. The system of teacher education which permitted trainee teachers to register for a full time specialist course on working with pupils with severe learning difficulties over three or four years, was terminated in the 1980s. Currently, all teachers must first qualify to teach in ordinary primary or secondary schools. After having completed a period of probationary teaching in ordinary schools, they may transfer to special schools and, if the funding is available, undertake a further period of full time or part time training. Irrespective of the advantages and drawbacks of a generic training, there is little doubt that teachers in special schools,who are initially trained for work in ordinary schools have very little preparation for, or experience of, dealing with the kinds of behaviours which are frequently displayed by pupils with severe learning disabilities. To this extent, they may be more sensitive to behaviours, which have the potential to challenge, than teachers who, in previous years, received a more focused training (Mittler 1993).

While there is no firm evidence to support the view that the number of pupils who present a challenge has increased, there is plenty of informal and anecdotal evidence to suggest that teachers and classroom support workers are more aware of pupils who present challenging behaviour than they were in the past. To the extent that a challenging behaviour represents a relationship between those who display the behaviour and those who interpret and respond to the behaviour, it would seem reasonable to conclude that the prevalence of challenging behaviour has increased; what remains unclear is whether this has arisen owing to changes in pupil behaviour or to changing demands, expectations and skills among carers and professionals.

Overview of this book

This book describes a research project which was set up to help teachers and classroom support staff to develop effective strategies for working with pupils who present challenging behaviours. All the project work was carried out in schools for pupils with severe learning difficulties. The research team comprised a teacher with many years experience of working with pupils with severe learning disabilities and a developmental psychologist with a special interest in education and people with disabilities. The aim of the project was not to train teachers in techniques but to work alongside teachers and classroom support workers in developing effective strategies which could be easily employed in schools. This book is based upon the original research report submitted to the Mental Health Foundation. The project also led to the development of a set of workshop training materials to assist in-service training in schools. These are published separately by the British Institute of Learning Disabilities.

In the rest of this introductory chapter we describe the objectives of the study and explain how they influenced the project methodology. We also explore some general issues concerned with school development programmes before summarising the main procedures we employed for working in schools. Chapter 2 takes a closer look at the literature on challenging behaviour including its prevalence and different approaches to intervention.

Before inviting schools to participate in intensive practical work designed to establish effective strategies for working with pupils who challenge, we conducted a preliminary survey of pupils with challenging behaviour in all special schools in the West Midlands; we present the results of this survey in Chapter 3. Chapter 4 describes the schools involved in the main part of the study and introduces the pupils who were selected for participation because of their challenging behaviour. We also provide background information on teachers' perceptions of the challenge presented by these pupils and prevailing methods of responding to challenging incidents.

Collaboration between staff in schools and the project team to develop improved strategies for working with pupils is described in Chapter 5. Chapter 6 considers how the agreed strategies were implemented. Chapter 7 describes the factors which facilitated or impeded implementation and presents the evidence for changes in pupil behaviours following the interventions. Further evaluations were conducted with class teachers, head teachers and classroom support workers at the end of the project and these are presented in Chapter 8. Finally, Chapter 9 provides a brief summary of the main findings and highlights implications for future research and practice.

AIMS AND OBJECTIVES OF THE STUDY

The aim of the study was to explore ways of supporting staff in SLD schools who work with pupils with challenging behaviours. This general aim was elaborated in three objectives:

(i) To collaborate with teachers and care staff in the design and implementation of a range of strategies for the management and amelioration of challenging behaviours in school settings. A basic tenet of the research is that collaboration implies a systematic approach to establish and maintain relationships between *researchers* and school staff which is significantly different from that which usually characterises researchers and their *subjects*.

(ii) To monitor and evaluate interventions and to identify those which can be most effectively employed in schools.

(iii) To develop in-service training which will assist teachers and other staff in working more effectively with pupils who present challenging behaviours.

Interventions as experiments

School intervention research is often based upon an experimental paradigm where researchers test presumed causal relationships between variables by manipulating input factors (independent variables) and observing the effect on significant outcomes (dependent variables). For example, in-service teacher education in maths might be regarded as an important determinant of maths teaching; teachers who receive the training become better maths teachers. The quality of maths teaching might also be regarded as having a direct causal relationship with pupil performance in maths. Pupils who are taught by teachers who have received training should perform better in maths than pupils taught by other teachers.

Figure 1.2 Intervention as experiments

Independent Variable	Dependent Variable
In-service training ⟶	Good practice in maths teaching
Good practice in maths teaching ⟶	Improved student performance in maths

The school based study described here can be represented in a similar way as a relationship between independent and dependent variables.

Independent Variables	Dependent Variable
School based collaboration with teachers and care staff ⟶	Improved methods of working with pupils who challenge
Improved methods of working with pupils who challenge ⟶	Lower levels of challenging behaviour

Experiments are usually carried out to establish an unambiguous relationship between the dependent and independent variables; at the conclusion of a successful experiment it should be possible to state whether or not the independent variable has a direct causal influence on the dependent variable.

However, there are many differences between schools and experimental laboratories. Perhaps the most important difference is that schools are complex social organisations in which adults and pupils interact in the pursuit of a range of educational objectives. It is, therefore, impossible to improve the discipline of a laboratory experiment in a school without, at the same time, disrupting the educational processes under investigation. Rather than conducting an experiment to establish the precise relationships between independent and dependent variables, the authors of this study were concerned with understanding the process of change which can lead to improved methods of working with pupils who present challenging behaviours. As such the project has a number of distinctive methodological features which are discussed briefly below

Collaboration with teachers

In *The New Meaning of Educational Change,* Fullan (1991) suggests that 'practical changes are those that address salient needs, that fit well with the teachers situation, that are focused and that indicate concrete 'how to do it' possibilities' (p.72). One way to discover whether there are approaches to working with pupils with challenging behaviours which meet these criteria and are also effective, is to carry out an intervention study in collaboration with teachers. We have used the term *collaboration* to indicate researchers and school staff working together as equal members of a team with a common purpose. We believe that teachers and researchers draw on complementary skills and experiences which are essential to the development of improved classroom practice. While the impetus for innovation and change came from the research team, there was little doubt that the subject of challenging behaviour was a 'salient need' for our colleagues in schools. Our common task was to establish effective intervention strategies which fitted well with the classroom situation and indicated 'concrete how to do it possibilities'. One test of the efficacy of this approach would be whether it became embedded in the culture and practice of the school to the extent that it endured after the completion of the project.

Figure 1.3 A Collaborative model for improving school practice

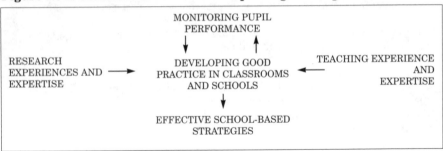

Monitoring and evaluation

There are many ways in which an attempt to change pupil behaviours may be evaluated. In this study we were concerned with a limited number of variables relating to the process of change and to the specific outcomes. These are:

(a) Measures of change in specific problem behaviours.

(b) Reducing the extent to which behaviours constitute a challenge. This may arise from a change in the behaviour itself or as a result of a management strategy which results in the behaviour having fewer challenging consequences. Challenging consequences are defined as follows:

- Reduced educational opportunities
- Isolation from peers
- Disruption of classroom activities
- Reduced access to community facilities

The collaborative approach outlined above suggests that other measures of outcome should also be included. For example, even when new methods of working prove effective, there will be few gains if teachers see them as difficult to implement in schools, or do not believe that they are effective or do not feel confident of their own abilities to continue employing them after the end of the project. For this reason, we have gathered information on the following:

- Satisfaction with the project methodology expressed by teachers and care staff.

- Perceived efficacy of the interventions agreed and introduced.

- Teachers' confidence in carrying the work forward.

In-service training

In-service training was identified as an objective for the staff directly involved in the study. It was anticipated that by being involved with the project team, staff would develop new ways of thinking about challenging behaviours and learn different response strategies. A longer term objective was the production of staff training materials which will enable staff in other schools to develop improved practice in respect of pupils with severe learning difficulties and challenging behaviours.

Process and Product

Insofar as the project was successful in developing new ways of working with pupils, staff development was an inevitable part of the process of collaboration. However, it was also important as an outcome for the project as a whole.

Towards the end of the period of direct involvement, each of the nine schools was offered a full day or half day INSET for all staff. A full day programme was arranged for five and a half day session was arranged for one school. Three schools either declined this invitation or were unable to alter an existing programme of staff training and development. In addition, three other schools the staff of which had heard of the project requested INSET support. These INSET days provided an important opportunity to field test and further develop training materials. Extensive revisions have been introduced and a final version is now available from The British Institute of Learning Disabilities. (Harris & Cook, 1995).

A whole school approach

Participation from all members of staff in the project which was considered appropriate for two reasons. First, if new ways of working with pupils with challenging behaviour were to become an accepted and self sustaining aspect of good practice, it was important to ensure that all members of staff knew and understood what was being undertaken. To quote Fullan, 'teachers who have a shared consensus about goals and the organisation of their work are more likely to incorporate new ideas' (p. 34). We hoped to establish such a shared consensus among all members of staff.

Secondly, we felt it was important to explore approaches which would increase rather than restrict pupils' involvement in activities throughout the school. If management strategies were to support the inclusion of pupils with challenging behaviours in a variety of educational and social activities, interaction with a range of adults throughout the school and diverse opportunities for learning, it was essential for all staff to be involved in the development and implementation of management strategies.

General issues in school development programmes

Fullan (1991) draws a number of conclusions from his review of research programmes designed to help schools to change. First, he differentiates 'real change' from acquiescence and token acceptance. Whereas it is relatively easy to talk about change and to agree a set of procedures for producing changes in schools, it is far from easy to implement those changes. The difficulty arises partly from the considerable difference in time scale between meetings which set out a programme for change and the long term process of making change happen. It also reflects the degree of commitment and effort which is required to move away from the comfort of well established routines and patterns of working to create new and possibly more demanding forms of professional practice.

Fullan refers to this sense of personal endeavour when he argues that for real changes to occur, teachers must alter the way in which they think about their work, 'Real change represents a serious personal and collective experience characterised by ambivalence and uncertainty'. However, he also suggests that there are significant benefits for teachers who succeed in producing change, 'If the change works out it can result in a sense of mastery, accomplishments and professional growth' (p. 32).

Thirdly, change is multi-dimensional and is likely to vary with both the individual teacher and the school. Thus, while it may be possible to plan change and to target specific objectives, the process by which change is achieved will involve numerous 'uncontrolled variables' (ranging from the personalities of those involved, additional unforeseen professional and personal demands, illness and staff turnover) and is, therefore, likely to be unpredictable. Outcomes will be attained to the extent that the change process is monitored and that adjustments are made as, and when, the need arises.

Fourthly, change consists of a dynamic inter-relationship which may involve new materials, new teaching approaches and the alteration of beliefs and attitudes. In this study, our primary objective was the development of improved methods of working with pupils who presented a challenge; to achieve this we encouraged teachers and their assistants to review the way in which they thought about inappropriate behaviour and to develop more positive attitudes about the scope for positive interventions; we also assisted with the development of new materials. Outcomes were dependent upon the extent to which the project team and groups of staff were able to develop and implement a common approach for responding to the challenge presented by individual pupils. Over and above these considerations, was the question of whether the specific interventions employed were appropriate to the needs of the pupils involved in the study.

Fifthly, change is a process which 'should be the result of adaptations and decisions made by users (teachers) as they work with new policies and programmes', (p. 38). The concept of change as a process which reflects the skills and experience of school staff was central to this project, and is set out in greater detail when we describe methods of working in school, in Chapter 4.

Given these parameters, the introduction of any form of change in schools is likely to be complex and potentially problematic. Of particular concern is the relationship which exists between external agents of change (in this case the research team) and the schools concerned.

'The difficulties in the relationship between external and internal groups are central to the problem and process of meaning. Not only is meaning hard to come by when two different worlds (for example, research and educational practice; clinical; psychology and teaching) have limited interaction, but misinterpretation, attribution of motives, feelings of being misunderstood and disillusionment on both sides are almost guaranteed'. (Fullan, 1991, p.80).

Having given such a gloomy prognostication for initiating school change, Fullan is rather more helpful regarding the best way to proceed. He suggests that school improvements are most likely when, 'teachers engage in continuous increasingly concrete and precise talk about teaching practice. Change involves learning to do something new and interaction is the primary basis for social learning' (p. 77). Furthermore, 'teachers say they learn best from other teachers, but research shows they interact with each other infrequently. When teachers are trained as staff developers, they can be very effective in working with other teachers. Teachers, also, say that they need direct outside help, if it is practical and concrete' (p. 85). He goes on to note that many school development programmes are unsuccessful as they do not provide in-service training during the period of implementation.

In this study, collaboration with schools and a 'whole school' approach was established in a number of ways. First, we were able to appoint a research officer with professional experience particularly relevant to this role. She had worked for many years as a teacher and deputy head in schools for pupils with severe learning difficulties and had developed a special interest in pupils with problematic or challenging behaviours. As a local authority advisory teacher, she had extensive experience in working alongside teachers in classrooms and in developing programmes of in-service training. Secondly, we chose to work with schools which responded to an initial screening questionnaire and indicated that they would welcome involvement from the project team. Thirdly, intervention was structured to promote dialogue among members of staff in the schools and between the school staff and the project team. Fourthly, the project addressed attitudes and beliefs as well as the development of new approaches and the introduction of new materials. Fifthly, intervention strategies were not offered as ready made programmes, but were developed as a result of observation and discussion. This process took place over a number of weeks and was designed to be responsive to the needs of individual pupils and their teachers, and to 'mesh' with the goals, values and practices of the different schools. Sixthly, the intervention programme specifically recognised the role of pupils and staff in wider social and organisational contexts such as the classroom, the school and the community.

Previous attempts to support schools working with pupils with challenging behaviour

When reporting on a school based study involving pupils with severe learning disabilities and challenging behaviours in the United States, Janey and Meyer (1990) reported, 'few examples of any kind investigating systematic efforts to address the broad range of student programming, staff development and resource utilisation needs implied by the general picture of apparent difficulty in providing integrated services to these students' (p. 187). A review of recent research in the UK confirms the absence of school-based work to address these issues directly. Janey and Meyer proposed a model which combined in-service training on theory, practice and the application of intervention strategies with on-site technical assistance from a team of experienced consultants. On average, school visits occurred for two hours during school time once every fortnight. During this time consultants met with staff to plan and 'problem solve'. They also demonstrated instructional techniques, designed curriculum and instructional modifications, and trained staff in specific strategies. For each student, consultants spent about forty hours in school during a twelve month period with a further three to four hours per week on preparation and report writing.

Working in institutional and community based settings in the United States, Durand and Kishi (1987) sought to provide staff with appropriate technical assistance to help them work with students with dual sensory impairments who presented problem behaviours. Two site visits were made. The first was used to assess targeted behaviours, establish data collection systems, train staff, implement treatment recommendations and video-tape staff and clients. The second visit, one month later, was designed to assess treatment gains and advise on any problems. A follow-up visit was made nine months later.

Assessment focused on the identification of the variables maintaining problem behaviours, functional skills, which could be developed, and potentially reinforcing events. Recommended interventions were initially implemented by consultants in the presence of staff. All the students were taught functional communication skills. Following these interventions, the authors report that three students showed immediate reductions in problem behaviours. For the other two students, problem behaviours did not initially change as staff had not implemented intervention procedures. Although the authors were able to intervene successfully with both these students during a site visit, staff were not able to maintain the treatment programme for one of them. The authors suggest that this result raises important questions about on-site support for staff who are asked to implement new strategies, the availability of staff time, the provision of constructive feedback and local contingencies (reinforcements) which make it rewarding for staff to continue working on an intensive programme.

A strategy for collaborative research: research procedures

In this section we summarise the design of the study and the procedures employed. Chapter 5 provides a more detailed account of the schools, the teachers and the pupils who participated in the study together with a description of how the procedures worked in practice.

Selecting schools

Initially, 44 schools in the West Midlands which make provision for pupils with severe learning difficulties were surveyed using a postal questionnaire. This was intended as a preliminary screening exercise to determine which schools were serving children who presented a challenge owing to their behaviour. The information obtained from the questionnaire is presented in Chapter 3. Using the information from the survey, a short list of schools was drawn up using the following criteria:

(i) They provided solely or mainly for pupils with learning difficulties.

(ii) They were located within a radius of twenty miles of the research base at the University of Birmingham.

(iii) They had completed the questionnaire and had identified a number of pupils with challenging behaviours which they felt unable to address.

(iv) When visited by the project staff, they expressed enthusiasm for, and a commitment to, the aims of the project.

(v) Local authority advisors and inspectors expressed their support for the school's inclusion in the project.

(vi) The schools had a relatively stable management structure (senior staff in post and no obvious signs of internal friction) and no other school development programmes which might compromise collaboration.

Work in schools

The work was carried out in two phases. This permitted intensive work within individual schools and the inclusion of nine schools overall. It was also intended that collaborative methods and strategies for addressing problem behaviour developed in the first phase schools would be refined and further evaluated in the second phase schools.

Phase I schools

Five schools were contacted and invited to participate in the first phase of the study. Seven specific objectives were identified for work in Phase I:

(i) Identify the types of behaviour which were perceived as challenging.

(ii) Determine the frequency and severity of problem behaviours.

(iii) Determine the social and educational consequences of those behaviours for the pupils, their peers and teachers.

(iv) Describe staff responses to problem behaviours.

(v) Collaborate with staff in developing strategies for intervention.

(vi)   Assist staff in implementing new approaches.

(vii) Enable staff to acquire knowledge, attitudes and skills which would provide the foundation for improved practice and ongoing development.

Phase I lasted from March to December 1992.

Phase II schools

Only four schools participated in Phase II, although a total of six were approached. The reasons for non-participation concerned impending staff changes (one school) and another development programme which was likely to take up significant amounts of staff time. The specific objectives for Phase II were:

(i)   Evaluate the methods of collaborative working and the intervention strategies developed in Phase I.

(ii) Explore the implications of working over a shorter time scale and providing less intensive support.

(iii) To refine the programme of in-service development and to produce a training programme for staff in other schools.

Phase II lasted from January to May 1993.

Procedures for collaboration and the provision of consultancy support

After making contact with each school by telephone and a preliminary visit, the project team proposed a schedule of visits and activities designed to meet the objectives detailed above. In essence, the model adopted was one of developing intervention to meet the needs of individual pupils and then exploring ways in which the proposed strategies could be integrated within the classroom and the school. Teachers and support staff who worked directly with selected pupils were the main change agents although the method of collaborative working was specifically designed to involve other members of staff including the senior managers.

The procedures employed were as follows:

1.   A whole school meeting was held to introduce all the staff to the aims of the project and outline proposed methods of working. The concept of challenging behaviour was introduced and staff were asked to identify pupils who presented behaviours which met the interpretative criteria set out in Chapter 2.

2.   The project research officer visited the school and initiated data collection. For Phase I schools, this involved the following elements:

- A detailed semi-structured interview with teachers responsible for selected pupils. A copy of the interview schedule is provided in Appendix 1. This provided a topographical description of the behaviours concerned together with the interpretative criteria on which the judgment of 'challenging' was made. Respondents were asked to rank the behaviours in terms of 'the challenge' they presented. This was used to establish priorities for observation and record keeping.

- Classroom observation, referred to as 'shadowing'.

- Teacher records of designated behaviours.

- The survey form of the Vineland Adaptive Behaviour Scale (Sparrow, Balla and Cicchetti 1984) was completed with teachers as the primary source.

For Phase II schools, a self-report questionnaire was employed instead of the interview. This was intended to save time and explore whether teachers could provide equivalent information without a face to face interview. A copy of the self report questionnaire is provided in Appendix 1.

3.   Pupil reviews were conducted to ascertain what was known about the pupil and the behaviours which were causing concern. Present at the review were the project team, the class teacher and (where possible) the support staff concerned, and the head teacher or deputy head teacher. The reviews were loosely structured around six key questions:

- How do you think the situation (i.e. what happens during an episode of problem behaviour) appears to this pupil?

- What do you think this pupil's needs are at this point?

- How are the present strategies helping?

- What are the problems associated with the present strategies?

- How do you think this pupil's needs can be met?

- What structures need to be in place in school for this pupil's needs to be met?

The outcome of the review was a summary paper which included the following information:

Pupil's name, age and sex
The main challenging behaviours
Other factors (for example, medical condition or adverse home situation)
Previous interventions
Recommendations of the review meeting
Specific strategies to be employed.

This document provided the basis for subsequent interventions.

4. One member of the project team adopted a consultancy role during the period of implementation. Regular visits to each school were scheduled, but she was also able to respond to requests for advice and support at other times. The consultancy role involved working with teachers to achieve the following:

    *   consideration of how recommendations could best be incorporated into existing classroom practice;

    *   organisational changes which would support or facilitate intervention procedures;

    *   involvement of other members of classroom staff;

    *   communication with other staff in the classroom and in other parts of the school;

    *   liaison with other professionals;

    *   consistent implementation of review recommendations throughout the school.

    In addition to working alongside teachers and support staff directly responsible for the selected pupils, her role included liaison with the head teacher and exploring ways in which good practice could be extended to other teaching and non-teaching staff. The number of visits to each school ranged from 20 to 29 with an average of 23. Apart from the initial visit, which usually lasted a whole day, most visits lasted approximately half a day.

5. The interventions with individual pupils were not formally terminated, although consultancy support was tapered and eventually withdrawn. Further classroom observations were carried out and teachers were asked to conduct post intervention monitoring of specific behaviours. Information on the duration and timing of pre - and - post intervention data collection is provided in appendix 2.

6. Following the post-intervention data collection, another whole school meeting was arranged. This took the form of an in-service session lasting either a half or a full day. In this session, an overview of the whole project was provided together with suggestions regarding the further development of a whole school approach to working with pupils who present challenging behaviours.

Measuring outcomes

Here, we briefly summarise the specific research questions which relate to outcomes and indicate the sources of data available to address these questions. Other questions, such as the most effective ways of working with teachers and the factors which affect implementation of agreed strategies, relate to the *process* of change and are dealt with descriptively in Chapter 6.

Summary of outcome measures

Variable	*Method of Data Collection*
What behaviours are considered challenging?	Survey questionnaire Semi-structured interview (Phase I) Self report questionnaire (Phase II)
Frequency, duration and severity of behaviours	Semi-structured interview (Phase I) Self report questionnaire (Phase II)
Social and educational consequence of problem behaviours	Semi-structured interview (Phase I) Self report questionnaire (Phase II)
Staff responses to problem behaviours	Semi-structured interview (Phase I) Self report questionnaire (Phase II) Classroom observation
Evidence for changes in pupil behaviours following the intervention	Classroom observation Teachers' records of problem behaviours
Evaluation by head teachers, class teachers and classroom assistants of the intervention programme	Post-intervention questionnaire

Chapter 2:

UNDERSTANDING CHALLENGING BEHAVIOURS

Definitions

Problem behaviours are usually described in one of two ways: *topographical descriptions* refer to actions performed and words spoken. They provide a relatively precise account of what it is that the child or adult does which causes concern. They may also provide information on the frequency of occurrence, average duration of behaviours and an estimate of intensity. *Interpretative descriptions* refer to the consequences of those actions for the person concerned and for other people. Most importantly, they include judgments about social context and the short and long term implications should the behaviours continue.

'Definitions' of challenging behaviours provide a set of interpretative statements for evaluating whether or not a behaviour is problematic or 'challenging'. A set of agreed interpretative criteria are helpful insofar as they encourage public discussion of subjective judgments and prevent the classification of behaviours as 'problems' merely because they are inconvenient or embarrassing. When interpretative criteria are used for making judgments about behaviour, not all instances of the same behavioural topography will be considered problematic. For example, running to get a bus does not constitute a challenge, but running around a classroom may well do so. Conversely, similar behaviours may be identified as presenting a 'challenge' for quite different reasons. For example, running may be regarded as disruptive when presented by a pupil in one setting but potentially dangerous in another.

Further information on behaviours which are frequently classified as 'problematic' or 'challenging" are provided in the discussion of prevalence. In this section we briefly summarise two interpretative statements.

Emerson, Barrett, Bell et al (1987) stated:

> 'By **severely challenging behaviour** we mean behaviour of such intensity, frequency or duration that the physical safety of the person or others is placed in serious jeopardy or behaviour which is likely seriously to limit or deny access to the use of ordinary community facilities. Ordinarily, we would expect the person to have shown the pattern of behaviour that presents such a challenge to services for a considerable period of time. **Severely challenging behaviour** is not a transient phenomenon'. (p. 8; emphasis in original).

Clements and Zarkowska (1988) suggest that a behaviour may legitimately be regarded as a problem if it satisfies some or all of the following criteria:

- The behaviour itself or its severity is inappropriate, given the person's age and level of development.

- The behaviour is dangerous either to the person himself or to others.

- The behaviour constitutes a significant additional handicap for the person by interfering with learning of new skills or by excluding the person from important learning opportunities.

- The behaviour causes significant stress to the lives of those who live and work with the person, and impairs the quality of their lives to an unreasonable degree.

- The behaviour is contrary to social norms.

First, it is important to recognise that these statements are not formal definitions, since they specifically invite further subjective judgments as part of the process of categorisation. For example, Emerson et al, rely heavily on 'seriousness' while Clements and Zarkowska suggest that behaviour may satisfy 'some or all' of their statements. However, the statements have been regarded as useful and are frequently employed as criteria for judging whether or not behaviours are problematic or challenging.

The statements cited above are useful for a number of reasons:

(i) They make explicit the distinction between a behaviour and its personal or social consequences.

(ii) They emphasise the interactive nature of problem behaviours, i.e. behaviours become 'problems' when they are fitted into a framework of social values and expectations.

(iii) They move the focus of responsibility away from the adult or child behaving 'badly' and toward environmental conditions which maintain the behaviour and social expectations, and permit its classification as 'problematic'.

(iv) Much has been made of the 'emotive' power of the term challenging; it suggests that difficult behaviours 'challenge' or 'test' the quality of service provision and places the onus on service staff to take up the challenge. (For example, recent publications from the King's Fund: *Facing the Challenge*, 1987; *Evaluating the Challenge*, 1991).

While accepting the rhetoric of the term 'challenging behaviour', the majority of surveys have been conducted using topographical descriptions of potentially problematic behaviours. The usual format is for respondents to be offered a list of specific behaviours and to be invited to identify those which fit a specific set of interpretative statements. The danger of this procedure is that respondents are heavily influenced by the list of behaviours and pay less attention to the interpretative statements. This would result in over reporting behaviours listed (including some that may not fit the interpretative criteria) and under reporting behaviours which fit the interpretative statements (because under local conditions they are problematic) but which are not on the list.

In the survey carried out as part of this study and when guiding teachers in the selection of pupils to participate in the intervention work, we have attempted to apply the notion of 'challenging behaviour' systematically by asking teachers to describe the behaviours which they regard as 'problematic'. We have provided an interpretative framework based on those of Emerson et al. and Clements and Zarkowska but we have relied upon teacher accounts of the behaviours which meet these criteria.

The development of strategies for intervention requires a more complete description of the behaviours concerned. In this study, before discussing possible interventions, behaviours identified by teachers as presenting a challenge were explored with reference to both their topographical features and the criteria against which they were evaluated.

The interpretative statement used in this study is as follows: 'The children under consideration are those whose behaviour within the context of your school:

- prevents participation in educational activities;

- isolates them from their peers;

- affects the learning of other pupils;

- drastically reduces their opportunities for involvement in ordinary community activities;

- makes excessive demands on staff and other resources; places the child or others in physical danger;

- threatens the prospects of future placement.'

Possible causes of challenging behaviours

In most cases, the precise cause of a behaviour which is regarded as problematic will remain unknown. A comprehensive analysis of causes would have to explain the complex interactions, over time, of biological predispositions; environmental factors such as diet and sensory stimulation; social experiences; and the child's growing ability to understand and interpret the world around.

However, there are occasions when it is helpful to think of more direct causes, for example, when a child who has an earache or begins to bang her head. In this section we summarise briefly, contributory factors which may be implicated in the emergence of challenging behaviours (Murphy & Oliver, 1987).

1. Children who are unable to communicate their needs and interests to others may become frustrated and resort to other responses. These actions may easily be interpreted as 'problems'; for example, pinching other children to obtain attention from an adult.

2. Some children with SLD may produce actions which result in various forms of stimulation; for example, hand flapping, eye poking or ear rubbing. Children with auditory disabilities are particularly likely to present stereotypic behaviours which have a self-stimulatory function.

3. Many children with SLD have a poorly developed sense of social rules and little understanding of the way in which their own behaviour affects other people. Children with autism, in particular, may present problematic behaviours which are inappropriate or socially embarrassing; for example, taking their clothes off in a public place when they are hot.

4. Parents and teachers sometimes unwittingly encourage inappropriate behaviours, for example, by providing extra attention in response to minor lapses in behaviour. After a time some children learn to attract attention by minor 'mis-behaviour'. Attempts by the adults to re-establish more acceptable behaviour, for example, by ignoring the child, may be met with an increase in intensity or duration of the inappropriate behaviour. If attention is given in response to behaviour of a given magnitude, it is likely that the adult behaviour, rather than reducing the strength of the 'challenge', will systematically 'shape up' more extreme forms of that behaviour. For example, the adult who initially refuses to respond to a child who whines for attention, but eventually gives in when the child begins to cry, may be inadvertently teaching the child that crying is rewarded with adult attention.

5. If children are educated in impoverished or unstimulating environments, challenging behaviours may occur in response to boredom and the absence of

structured opportunities to learn appropriate or adaptive behaviours.

6.   Some behaviours may be regarded as problematic because they are characteristic of children of a younger chronological age. In some cases, the immature behaviours may linger because they have been tolerated by adults who have not encouraged the development of more age-appropriate responses. Daytime soiling and wetting are examples.

7.   For some children there may be a more direct link between some physiological or neurological dysfunction and specific behaviours. For example, children with Prader Willi Syndrome are prone to excessive eating to the extent that their health is seriously impaired. A very high proportion of children with Lesch-Nyhan Syndrome self-injure and children with Rett Syndrome are prone to repetitive and inappropriate hand movements.

8.   Undiagnosed and untreated medical conditions may lead to pain or discomfort. Children who are unable to communicate are likely to respond with behaviours which may be interpreted as 'challenging'. If the discomfort continues, or if the behaviour leads to punitive responses from adults, a self-sustaining cycle of ever-increasing levels of 'difficult behaviour' may be established.

How many children with severe learning disabilities present a challenge?

A total population survey carried out by Quine (1986) in two health districts using the Disability Assessment Schedule (Holmes, Shah and Wing 1982) provides the most detailed recent study of school aged children with severe learning disabilities and challenging behaviours. The mean prevalence rates of children who had been, or were likely to be, assessed as suitable for education in ESN(s) schools increased from 1.48 per thousand for children 0-4, to 3.25 per thousand for those between 5 and 9. For those between 10 and 14 years of age the figures is slightly lower at 2.8 per thousand. This pattern and the overall prevalence rates are consistent with other studies (Kushlick & Cox 1968; Kidd 1964; Wing 1971). The teacher or care assistant who knew the child best was asked whether he or she had severe or mild behaviour problems which caused significant social or psychological disability to himself, herself or others. The main results are presented in Table 2.1.

More recently, Qureshi and Alborz (1992) reported a similar study across seven health districts in the north west of England which included 1057 children over the age of five, with severe learning disabilities, attending schools or living in residential homes. Instead of collecting information on discrete behaviours, they looked at the consequences for the children concerned and the responses of those who worked with them.

Table 2.1
Behaviour problems presented by children with severe learning disabilities (Quine, 1986)

	%	Boys N = 245 %	Girls N = 154 %	P
Attention seeking	29	30	29	NS
Overactive	21	25	14	0.01
Temper tantrums	25	27	21	NS
Aggression	21	23	17	NS
Screams	22	24	19	NS
Wanders	18	19	17	NS
Destructive	14	16	11	NS
Self-injuring	12	13	10	NS
N = 399				

Overall, 45% of children presented severe or mild behaviour problems

Preliminary screening criteria were:

* the provision of special resources to manage the behaviour;

* injury to self or others;

* damage to or destruction of the environment;

* severe social disruption which affected the quality of life of others.

On this basis, 27% of children in residential homes (total number = 205) and 10% of those in schools (total number = 1047) presented problem behaviours.

A more rigorous set of criteria was also applied:

* causing more than minor injury to themselves or others;

* destroying their immediate environment;

* causing disruption lasting more than a few minutes on at least a daily basis;

* behaviour which resulted in one or more of the following at least weekly: physical danger to self; intervention by more than one member of staff; disruption lasting an hour or more.

This resulted in a 5% prevalence rate for children in community services. No separate figures are provided for boys and for girls.

Children with severe learning disabilities are not a homogeneous population and a number of studies have been concerned with the extent to which the causes of the primary disability are associated with differential rates of problem behaviour. Gath and Gumley (1986) compared children aged 6-17 years of age with Down's Syndrome and matched groups of children with other diagnoses in one health authority in England. Parents and teachers were interviewed and asked to complete the Rutter Scales A2 and B2 respectively. There were no differences in the percentages of pupils with deviant scores (above 13) on the parent scale but the control children were more frequently found to have deviant scores (above 9) on the teacher scale. Both parent and teacher scores indicated more hyperactive behaviour among the control group of children. Overall, when the criterion of a high score on one of the Rutter scales and also a high score on the Additional Behaviour Checklist (Gath and Gumley, 1984) was used, 38.3% of the Down's Syndrome group and 49% of the control group were categorised as having severe behaviour problems. The difference between this figure and those reported by Quine and Qureshi is probably a reflection of the methodology and instrumentation employed.

In an Australian study, Cuskelly and Dadds (1992) compared the prevalence of behaviour problems among children with Down's Syndrome and their siblings. Fathers, mothers and teachers were invited to complete the Revised Behaviour Problem Checklist (Quay & Peterson, 1983). The data showed that children with Down's Syndrome presented significantly greater problems than their siblings. While mothers reported the same frequency of problem behaviours in boys as girls, fathers reported more problems for girls, and teachers indicated that boys presented more problems. While none of the mean scores for children with, or without, Down's Syndrome exceeded two standard deviations above the mean on the published norms, 38% of the children with Down's Syndrome and 43% of their siblings reached this criterion on at least one subscale from data provided by at least one rater.

Thus, there is some agreement that, when completing standardised checklists, teachers and parents identify nearly 40% of children with Down's Syndrome as presenting serious problem behaviours. However, there is also evidence that teachers and parents report somewhat different levels of problem behaviour. This may reflect differential behaviour patterns at home and at school. It may also arise from different expectations by teachers and parents about appropriate conduct and consequent variations in the interpretation and evaluation of potentially problematic behaviours.

Kiernan and Kiernan (1994) have recently reported a school based survey of pupils with severe learning difficulties who present challenging behaviours. They asked teachers to provide information on three areas of challenging behaviour: aggressive behaviour such as verbal abuse or spitting; destructive and disruptive behaviours which lowered the pupil's quality of life or interfered with their own education or that of others; behaviours such as stereotypic or ritualistic behaviours which interfered with educational interventions. Respondents were asked to classify the severity of the challenging behaviour on a four point scale ranging from *extremely* difficult to *least* difficult. From a total population of 400 day schools for pupils with severe learning difficulties in England and Wales, 137 were approached and analysable data were provided by 105 schools.

Table 2.2

Challenging behaviours presented by pupils in special schools (Kiernan & Kiernan, 1994)

Behaviours	Independently Mobile group N = 324 %	Not independently mobile group N = 43 %
Aggression	44	30
Social disruption	35	42
Temper tantrums	34	35
Physical disruption	32	21
Destructive behaviour	31	0
Self injury	30	49
Non-compliance	28	16
Rituals	24	21
Stereotyped behaviour	19	19
Wandering	20	0
Masturbation	15	0

N refers to those pupils who presented some form of challenging behaviour.

Of the total pupils included in the sample, 22.2% were identified as presenting one or more challenging behaviours. Just over 8% were rated *extremely* difficult or *very difficult*, with the remaining 14% classified as *less* difficult. There was a preponderance of boys in both groups (57% and 60.4% respectively) and a tendency for challenging behaviour to be associated with limited expressive language. The number of pupils identified increased with age up to the age of 16 but the proportion of these who were rated 'extremely difficult' or 'very difficult' varied from 48% at ages 14 years to 34% at ages 7-8 and 15-16 years (mean for all age bands 38%). The authors provide a breakdown of the types of challenging behaviour presented by those pupils who were independently mobile and those who needed some form of mobility aide. Table 2.2 shows the data for the pupils rated extremely difficult, or very difficult.

The ratings provided by the schools of the seriousness of these behaviours was checked using a discriminant function analysis. Under-estimation of the seriousness of the management problems presented by pupils was found for only 28 cases (3.2%) while overestimation of the severity of pupils' problems was found in only eight cases (0.9%). This suggests that staff in schools were reasonably consistent in categorising pupils as more or less difficult in respect of the challenging behaviours they presented. When asked to indicate the reasons for pupils' problem behaviours, the most frequent responses were attention seeking (35%), demand avoidance (27%), communication problems (26%), stress (22%), interference with routines (18%) and provocation (17%). The challenging behaviour presented by a further 21% of pupils was regarded as unpredictable.

Self injury

Self injurious behaviour is not restricted to adults and children with learning disabilities (Winchel & Stanley, 1991) and Putnam and Stein (1985) describe eleven different conditions arising in childhood which are associated with self injury. However, self injury is one of the most common and distressing forms of challenging behaviour among adults and children with severe learning disabilities (Emerson, 1992).

Oliver Murphy and Corbett (1987) defined self injury as 'repeated self-inflicted non-accidental injury, producing bruising or bleeding or other temporary or permanent tissue damage and any such behaviour which would produce tissue damage were it not for protective devices, restraints, specific medical or psychological interventions in use' (p. 148). They found 596 cases of self injury among all people known to mental handicap services in one health region, giving a prevalence for people in hospital of 12% and for people attending social education centres of 3%. For children attending ESN(s) schools the prevalence was 3% for 0-5 year olds, 4% for 5-10 year olds and 12% for those over 15 years of age.

The most commonly reported self injurious behaviours were skin picking (39%), self-biting (38%), head punching or slapping (36%), head to object banging (28%), body to object banging (10%). Head to object banding, head punching and digit chewing were relatively more common among younger age groups while skin picking and self mutilation with tools were less common than would be expected. Younger children were more likely to present more than one self injurious behaviour. The prevalence and topography of SIB was not related to the sex of the people studied. Seventy five people wore protective devices or were physically restrained to prevent self injury and 44% were receiving psychotropic medication. Only twelve people were receiving psychological programmes of treatment.

In a study of twenty-one London schools serving pupils with severe learning difficulties, Gabony (1991) identified 113 cases of self injury. Apart from one behaviour (kicking own legs), there were no sex effects but, like Oliver et al., he found head banging against objects to be more prevalent among younger pupils. Over 72% of those pupils with SIB aged 2-7 years, presented this behaviour. Children who had 'some degree of communicative ability' were more prone to hand punch or slap, bang their body with a hand or arm and skin picking or peeling.

A survey carried out in the United States examined the frequency of self injury among students with mental retardation (learning disability), autism and additional handicaps (Griffin, Ricketts, Williams at al. 1987). Self injury was identified as repetitive or isolated acts towards oneself that resulted in physical harm, such as bleeding, bruises or broken bones, or similar acts that did not cause harm but were 'typically considered to represent a self injurious behaviour response'. Individuals who were restrained or who received medication as treatment for self injury were also included. Of the 2663 students surveyed, 2.6% exhibited at least one of these types of self injury during the preceding twelve months. The most frequently reported self injurious behaviours were biting (46%), head hitting (42%), head banging (30%), scratching (24%), arm hitting (20%), eye gouging (14%), hair pulling (14%), orifice digging (13%), mouthing (11%), ruminating (10%). The behaviours are similar to those found in other studies which included institutional populations (see Oliver et al, 1987), while the overall prevalence for self injury (2.6%) is consistent with that found by Kiernan and Kiernan in their study of school students in Britain.

There were slightly more males (59%) compared to females (41%) and self injury was more common among younger students although insufficient data are presented to evaluate this in relation to the underlying age distribution of students. Over 82% of those identified were rated as severely or profoundly retarded with only 17% mildly or moderately retarded. More than 50% of the students had been physically restrained at least once in the preceding twelve month period.

Summary

Various authors have proposed criteria which can be used to make judgments about which behaviours are challenging and why. These include a consideration of the risks of injury to the person concerned or to others, the extent to which the behaviour interferes with the provision of care and education, and judgments about 'appropriateness' given the person's age and level of development. While these criteria do not offer formal definitions of challenging behaviours, they do provide a number of potential safeguards:

- Negative judgments ('bad behaviour') require justification

- The reasons underlying the judgment can be made explicit

- The implications **if no action is taken** are clear.

The distinction between the form or topography of the behaviour and the challenge it may present is extremely important. All behaviours occur in relation to particular settings and activities. Judgments about behaviours are made in relation to our expectations about what is relevant and appropriate to those settings and activities. Similar behaviours may be judged more or less challenging depending on what is regarded as relevant and appropriate to different settings. And, of course, quite different behaviours may be judged challenging by reference to the same criteria.

For parents, teachers and care staff, it is distressing and frustrating when a child behaves in ways which seem to make little or no sense. Failure to change the behaviour suggests that we don't understand why the behaviour occurs; because the cause of the behaviour is elusive, it is impossible to determine the most effective treatment.

Understanding why particular children present challenging behaviours is a major task. It is complicated because the criteria we use to make judgments about the behaviour (in terms of the undesirable implications if no action is taken) have no systematic relationship with the causes of the behaviour. Pupils do not have temper tantrums in order to put their peers at risk of injury, although this may well be one of the consequences. Rather than looking at the implications of the behaviour from the point of view of concerned adults, we need to develop a perspective which incorporates the pupil's understanding of his or her place in the world and the limited opportunities which are available to exert control and influence other people. Inevitably, this is a daunting task when working with pupils who have severe learning disabilities.

While we have reviewed some of the possible causes of challenging behaviours, it would be unwise to consider this list as anywhere near complete. These and other causes may operate singly or in combination to produce behaviours which are viewed as challenging. Effective school-based intervention will require procedures which help teachers and care staff to develop an understanding of the factors contributing to the challenge presented by each individual child.

Research on children with learning disabilities who present challenging behaviours shows that the most frequently reported challenging behaviours are aggression towards others, destruction of property, disruption of classroom activities and socially inappropriate behaviours. Estimates vary, depending upon the way in which challenging behaviours are defined and measured, but it seems likely that, in many schools, as many as 20% of pupils will present some form of challenge (Kiernan and Kiernan 1994). Self injury is a particularly distressing form of challenging behaviour displayed by between 3% and 12% of all children with severe learning disabilities (Oliver *et al*, 1987).

Chapter 3

STRATEGIES FOR WORKING WITH PUPILS WHO PRESENT CHALLENGING BEHAVIOURS

In this chapter we provide an overview of different strategies advocated for use by those working with adults and children who present challenging behaviours. Inevitably, the work in schools described later in this report drew on a number of well known theoretical perspectives and a variety of practical interventions described in the research literature and professional journals. Our objective was not to invent new methods but to explore with teachers how their classroom practice could be improved in the light of current knowledge. The review begins with a summary of recent developments in behavioural methods before considering other approaches.*

Behavioural approaches

For many years behaviour modification has provided the cornerstone of most systematic attempts to overcome problem behaviours. Central to this approach is the distinction between behaviour and any interpretation of internal states or motives which may have *caused* the behaviour. The behavioural approach provides us with the tools for changing what people do, but not what they think, feel or believe. All behaviour is seen as being directly related to the events which precede and follow it; events which regularly occur before the behaviour are seen as having a triggering or cueing function while events which reliably follow a behaviour determine the consequences or 'pay off'. When the consequences result in favourable outcomes, they are referred to as 'reinforcing' events; if behaviours are repeatedly followed by reinforcing events, the behaviours will tend to happen more often, for a longer duration and with greater intensity. When the events which follow behaviours are unfavourable, they are described as punishing; when behaviours are constantly followed by punishing events, the behaviours will tend to occur less frequently and have shorter duration and a lower intensity.

The predictable relationships which exist between behaviours and contingent events in the environment provides the basis for the sophisticated technology known as behaviour therapy.

Strategies for reducing challenging behaviours

The most obvious application of behaviour therapy to challenging behaviours has been the elaboration of strategies which permit behaviour to be followed with the presentation of a punishing event or the removal of a positively reinforcing

---

* Parts of this review appear in J. Harris, M. Cook & G. Upton (1993) 'Challenging Behaviour in the Classroom', in J.Harris (ed). *Innovations in the Education of Pupils with Severe Learning Difficulties*. Chorley, Lancs: Lisieux Hall.

event; in either case, the person presenting the behaviour is faced with an unfavourable outcome which ought to lead to a reduction in the strength of the challenging behaviour.

Behaviour reduction strategies employed in the United States include:

1. Simple punishment: brief faradic shock delivered to the skin; a disagreeable tasting substance placed in the person's mouth; air or water sprayed to the face; ammonia salts placed under the person's nose.

2. Over-correction: repetition of desirable behaviours which include clearing up or making amends for consequences of disruptive behaviour.

3. Contingent restraint: the person is physically restrained after presenting a challenging behaviour.

4. Facial screening: the person's vision is blocked following a challenging behaviour.

5. Time out: the person is placed in a barren environment where they are systematically deprived of the opportunities for positive reinforcement.

6. Response cost: the person loses points, tokens or privileges consequent to performing a challenging behaviour,

7. Verbal reprimand.

8. Extinction: the reinforcement(s) that have previously maintained the challenging behaviour are removed.

Such approaches have been subjected to increasing criticism in recent years and have been described as dehumanising and unethical (Horner, Dunlop, Koegel et al, 1990). Their efficacy has been called into question because they require little detailed analysis of the relationships which may exist between the behaviours and a variety of environmental antecedents and consequences; use of punishment procedures does not lead us to ask why the behaviours are occurring. More recently, it has become clear that there are alternative approaches which, instead of focusing on reducing undesirable behaviours, ask how challenging behaviour may be overcome by encouraging positive, more appropriate behaviours.

Alternatives to punishment

There are a number of strategies which, when used singly or in combination, can effectively overcome challenging behaviour without the use of punishment or the removal of reinforcing events found in ordinary environments. They include:

1. Changing antecedent or setting conditions in order that the cues which elicit the challenging behaviours are no longer presented, or introducing competing cues which are associated with performance of more appropriate behaviours (Horner et al, 1990, Luiselli, 1990).

2. The application of differential schedules of reinforcement (Horner et al, 1990; O'Brien & Repp, 1990). In this procedure, appropriate behaviours are encouraged and strengthened by the presentation of reinforcers and, simultaneously, undesirable or challenging behaviours are denied reinforcers so that they become weaker and gradually die out. Among the most common of these differential schedules are:

   DRO   the differential reinforcement of other (non-challenging) behaviours; this is equivalent to reinforcing the person for not performing a challenging behaviour.

   DRA   the differential reinforcement of an alternative behaviour, i.e. reinforcing a non-challenging behaviour even though occasionally a challenging behaviour still occurs.

   DRI   the differential reinforcement of a behaviour which is incompatible with challenging behaviour, i.e. it is physically impossible for the person to perform the target behaviour and the challenging behaviour together.

   DRL   reinforcement is delivered when the frequency of the challenging behaviour does not exceed a pre-specified low level response.

3. Modifying more general environmental or ecological factors such as diet, eating schedules, opportunities for exercise, sleeping patterns, noise levels and the predictability of daily events.

4. Creating a positive lifestyle including access to a range of activities, places, people and events.

5. Improving social competence with training designed to support compliance to verbal and non-verbal commands, communicative competence and independence (Luiselli, 1990; Horner et al., 1990. O'Brien & Repp 1990).

There is also widespread support for the view that adults and children who present severe challenging behaviour are most effectively helped by intervention strategies which include a number of discrete components each of which is selected to address a clearly identified need or deficit. For example, Fox (1990) describes a programme designed to help an institutionalised young man aged 22 with severe learning disabilities.

Because of severe and prolonged self injury, physical restraints including arm splints and a face mask had been used regularly since he was an infant. The programme included four separate components:

(i) DRO: reinforcement for intervals during which self injury did not occur.

(ii) The gradual removal of physical restraints using a fading procedure.

(iii) Reinforcing appropriate non-challenging behaviours.

(iv) The provision of vocational training to increase the range of 'ordinary life' options available and promote a more positive lifestyle.

(For a readable summary of positive behavioural approaches for helping people with challenging behaviours see Donnellan, LaVigna, Negri-Shoultz and Fassbender,1988).

Challenging behaviour and communication

There is now substantial support for the view that effective remedial intervention for pupils with challenging behaviour rests on our ability to specify the functional relationship which exists between the behaviour and events which occur before and afterwards (Iwatta, Pace, Kalsher et al, 1990). To overcome challenging behaviours it is necessary to understand why they occur (Repp, Felce and Barton, 1988). As we have already seen, similar behaviours may operate in different ways for different pupils and a pupil may present a behaviour which has different functions in different settings. This suggests that it is helpful to classify challenging behaviours according to the purpose they serve and the outcomes they produce rather than their form or topography. More importantly, it has been suggested that effective interventions might involve helping a pupil to learn new, more acceptable behaviours, which can replace challenging behaviours because they help the pupil attain the same, or very similar, outcomes to those previously associated with the performance of challenging behaviours.

Carr and Durand (1985) suggest that most challenging behaviours fall into one of two functional categories: escape behaviours, which are maintained by the reinforcing effects of avoidance; and attention-seeking behaviours, which are maintained by positive reinforcement. To demonstrate the effect of replacing challenging behaviours by functionally equivalent communicative behaviours, they taught simple phrases to three pupils who presented a variety of aggressive, self-destructive and disruptive behaviours. For example, one pupil whose behaviour was analysed as having an escape function, was taught to elicit help by saying, 'I don't understand', and the teacher replied 'OK, I'll show you'. Another pupil was taught to say 'Am I doing good work?' and the teacher replied, 'I like the way you are working today. You're putting all the pictures where they belong'. Levels of disruptive behaviours fell dramatically following the communication training.

In another study, Dyer and Dunlap (1990) worked with three pupils who presented aggression, self injury and temper tantrums. Levels of problem behaviour (biting, hitting, kicking, pinching; throwing, tearing, and banging objects; screaming, whining and crying) were significantly reduced after they were taught to express choices and encouraged to use materials during structured teaching sessions.

Both of these studies suggest that at least some challenging behaviours reflect a pupil's inability to interact in a positive and meaningful way with the environment. When the pupils were provided with the skills and opportunities to influence their environment there were substantial reductions in the levels of challenging behaviours.

Taken one step further, it is possible to see challenging behaviours as having a somewhat broader range of functions which are equivalent to the following messages:

- Pay attention to me

- I want ......

- I don't need this any more.

- I need help.

- I am bored.

- I am tense, anxious, overwhelmed.

- I am frightened.

- I am hurt.

- I don't feel well. (Donnellan, Mirenda, Mesaros et al, 1984).

Underlying this approach is the belief that pupils with challenging behaviour are struggling to make sense of a complex and sometimes frightening environment. Challenging behaviours become established because they provide the pupil with a significant element of control in situations where he or she would otherwise be relatively powerless. Furthermore, challenging behaviours are not particularly effective ways of communicating; adult responses are to some extent variable and inconsistent. As a result, they provide the pupil with few opportunities to experience the power and potential complexity of simple two-way communicative interactions. On the other hand, they are effective precisely because they are perceived by adults as presenting a challenge and, to the extent that the pupil can increase the frequency, intensity or duration of the behaviours, sooner or later an adult response will be forthcoming. (For a practical guide to communication training for pupils with challenging behaviour, see Durand, 1990).

Person-centred approaches

Educationalists and clinical psychologists committed to the behavioural approach have sought to establish non-aversive ways of helping pupils who present challenging behaviours. Rather than attempting to suppress or reduce the level of inappropriate behaviours directly, they ask whether behavioural techniques can be used in a more positive manner, for example, can pupils be taught to employ appropriate behaviours in place of those which are seen as challenging (Durand, 1990).

However, for some clinicians, the reservations about behavioural programming go much deeper. In particular, they are critical of the way in which behavioural approaches can inhibit the development of meaningful human relationships and lead to 'treatments' which take no account of the 'subject's' interests and personal motivation. In the following sections, we briefly consider two alternative approaches to working with people who present challenging behaviours. Both have been employed extensively with adults, but rather less with pupils. However, the under-lying rationale and approach to intervention is clearly relevant to work with children and adolescents in schools.

A counselling approach

Lovett (1985) argues that his overall aim in working with people who have special needs is to 'give them the freedom of choice and the dignity of risk' (p. 30). This involves asking questions about the function of behaviour: 'How does the way a person acts help them?' (p. 34). Instead of carrying out an analysis of the inter-relationships between a person's behaviour and various environmental contingencies, Lovett relies upon human inter-subjectivity, even if this means making intuitive judgments about underlying motives.

> 'When a person does something, I am not uncomfortable asking what it means to her. If she finds acting that way uncomfortable, then I look for ways she can learn another way. My experience is that this allows me to build a working relationship rather than exert my trained will on a "problem behaviour". (p. 38).

> When we work with persons who cannot express themselves clearly except through the way they act, we are always guessing what these actions mean and what ways will help them express themselves more effectively'. (p. 67).

Using a series of case studies, Lovett illustrates how this approach can work in practice. His central theme is the need to use our subjective knowledge about our own behaviour to understand the behaviour of others. When trying to help someone whose behaviour is inappropriate or unpleasant he recommends asking the following questions:

- How do I feel when this happens?

- In what sort of position or with what way of looking at the world would I find acting like this helpful?

- How would I like to be approached if I found this strategy satisfying while those around me did not?

The answers are then explored through interactions which seek to replicate ordinary relationships. The goal is to help the person see that they can choose to act differently and, by taking a decision to change their behaviour towards others, they are likely to benefit from more meaningful and satisfying relationships. Sometimes people may need considerable help, not because they do not wish to change, or because they do not want to develop relationships, but because they have never learned how to interact with others.

'We sometimes forget that learning how to have relationships is learned; they are not simply instinctual. When a person acts 'bizarrely' this is often the result of her being unaware of the social consequences or being frightened about how to manage a social situation successfully. This is a skills deficit we commonly overlook' (Lovett 1985, p. 44).

Gentle teaching
Like Lovett, the proponents of Gentle Teaching (McGee, Menolascino, Hobbs and Menousek, 1987) regard the development of human relationships as central to effective interventions for people who present behavioural challenges. 'It is essential to teach that there is a value and goodness in human interactions, human presence and human participation' (p. 19). This can be difficult, especially where people have experienced a range of unpleasant and aversive treatments which are 'toxic' to the development of meaningful relationships. To overcome initial hostility and fear it is necessary to show that:

- Our presence signals safety and security

- Our words and contacts are inherently rewarding

- Participation leads to reward.

To achieve this, those who seek to help must accept and value the presence of the person with 'even the most despicable behaviours' so that reward giving and sharing become associated with being among other people. Note that, in this context, McGee et al (1987) use the term 'reward' or 'human reward' to describe human interactions which communicate value, equality and acceptance. Tasks are only employed as a context or framework to facilitate interactions, not because of any intrinsic value attached to learning new skills.

The teacher or therapist should be guided by the following questions:

- How can I make human reward the central focus, purpose and outcome of our interactions?
- How does my teaching support and facilitate this focus and purpose?
- How can I defuse and re-direct inequitable interactional responses?

Three specific strategies are advocated by McGee et al (1987):

Ignoring involves 'acting as if the behaviour had not occurred'. By ignoring, the teacher gives as little value as possible to the disruptive or destructive behaviour.

Redirecting means guiding the person towards interactions which can bring about human reward. The underlying message which is communicated should be 'Here, do this instead'.

Interruption involves picking up signs of impending aggression or disruption and redirecting the person before it happens.

These strategies should be co-ordinated so that a continuous interaction is possible, even when a person presents problem behaviour. Low level challenges might be overcome using the sequence: ignore - redirect - reward. Other more intense behaviours such as physical aggression or self injury, may require more overt action: interrupt - ignore - redirect - reward.

McGee et al (1987) suggest a number of practical steps to be taken when confronted by different kinds of behavioural challenge. The approach is illustrated here in connection with aggression and temper tantrums or 'furies'.

Practical techniques for responding to aggression:
- protect yourself unobtrusively

- say nothing about it

- calmly redirect the person to the task

- use gesture and physical assistance

- demonstrate concrete instructional goals
- give strong reward

- continue re-direction

Practical techniques for responding to temper tantrums:

- calm the person in a non-obtrusive manner and try to redirect

- protect yourself, the person and others

- do not chastise the person; remain calm and soothing

- redirect the person to the task or activity

- as the person redirects, focus on participation and reward

- in future focus on prevention

- try to redirect as precursors appear

Both Lovett's counselling approach and Gentle Teaching are relatively new approaches to working with people who present challenging behaviours. Very little systematic evaluation has been carried out on Lovett's work and the studies which have been undertaken to examine the effectiveness of Gentle Teaching have not yet proved conclusive (McGaughey & Jones, 1992). However, there is no doubt that, for many parents and professionals, they have an intuitive appeal and are likely to continue to exercise a strong influence, particularly on those who are disillusioned with behavioural intervention strategies.

What is effective intervention?
As the sophistication of treatment strategies has increased, so the question of what counts as effective intervention has become more difficult to answer. For example, there is a *prima facie* case for regarding a decrease in the frequency, duration or intensity of a challenging behaviour as being both a necessary and sufficient condition to determine the success of any intervention. Unfortunately, this provides only a very restricted view of a more complex picture. The focus on specific behaviours is but a

means to a more general end: the attempt to provide pupils with severe learning disabilities with experiences which will enable them to grow and develop and to take their place as valued members of the community. If interventions which result in short term gains or in the substitution of one problem behaviour for another, possibly a more challenging alternative, are to be properly evaluated, it is important to keep in mind this broader context.

Traditionally, experimental psychology has been concerned with establishing causal links between an independent variable, such as a treatment, and a relevant outcome measure, such as a targeted behaviour. A treatment is regarded as valid when it is possible to demonstrate that the outcome measures change as a result of a specific intervention. Complications arise as soon as we ask, 'What counts as a relevant outcome measure?'. Moreover, the number of relevant outcomes increase when treatment takes place, not in a laboratory or a clinic but in a *real life* setting such as a school.

> 'As long as our notions of what constitutes 'effectiveness' are restricted to demonstrations of experimental control over single target behaviours in treatment environments, both science and practice can be regarded as contributing to the restrictions placed upon the lives of persons with severe disabilities' (Myer & Janney, 1989, p. 264).

The effectiveness of any treatment can be interpreted in a number of quite different ways:

1. Does the treatment *per se* produce the desired effects under optimal conditions, for example, in a laboratory or a clinic setting? Have any possible effects of extraneous factors, for example, changes in conditions at home, been ruled out as contributory factors? This is often referred to as the question of internal validity (Campbell & Stanley, 1968).

2. Is the treatment effect robust enough to produce similar effects when employed elsewhere, for example, by other psychologists or teachers working with children who present similar problems? This is referred to as external validity (Campbell & Stanley, 1968).

3. What happens when the setting is changed from the laboratory or clinic to a real life setting? Is it still possible to provide the treatment in a way which produces predictable changes in the outcome measure? This is a question of ecological validity.

4. Finally, it may be asked whether the treatment produces outcomes which are recognised as being socially important and whether the treatment process is

justified in terms of what is achieved. This is the question of social validity (Wolf, 1978).

School-based research which explores new ways of working with pupils who present challenging behaviours is likely to be concerned with all four aspects of validity. It is desirable to demonstrate that treatments produce specific effects and that effective strategies may be generalised to other teachers and pupils. Treatments will only be seen as useful in the long term to the extent that they work within schools and do not depend upon the introduction of artificial procedures which undermine legitimate educational activities and routines. Finally, the objectives should be regarded as worthwhile and the means by which they are achieved should be acceptable to school staff, parents and pupils.

With this in mind, potential outcome measures are increased considerably. Myer and Janney (1989) suggest the following:

1. Changes in the frequency, duration or intensity of the target behaviour.

2. Changes in other inappropriate behaviours, in addition to, or instead of, those targeted.

3. The acquisition of adaptive behaviours such as new skills or strategies for self control.

4. Behaviour changes across settings and people, for example, are the changes consistent in respect of different activities and different teachers?

5. The level of involvement in group activities and inclusion in extracurricular events.

6. Access to a curriculum which meets educational and developmental needs.

7. A reduced need for medical services and/or crisis management.

8. Subjective 'quality of life' measures: happiness, satisfaction, ability to make choices and take control.

9. Perceptions of improvement by staff and family.

10. Expanded social relationships.

To this might be added measures relating to the acceptability of intervention strategies for school staff members and the ease with which they can be employed without disrupting other valued activities (Tarnowski, Mulick and Rasnake, 1990).

Needless to say, as the implementation of treatments becomes more difficult and problematical when they are transferred to real life settings, the technical problems involved in measuring outcomes multiply. It is worth emphasising that the available evidence suggests that positive outcomes are more likely to be achieved with treatment programmes which involve a number of related components; consequently, measures of efficacy will reflect the treatment package as a whole rather than individual elements within it.

To the extent that intervention is carried out by practitioners who must, simultaneously, carry out a range of other professional tasks, treatment effects will inevitably be conflated with and contaminated by a variety of everyday activities and interactions. In this study, we were not concerned with the changes which would have to be introduced in schools to enable teachers to operate sophisticated treatment programmes, but with helping teachers to develop and extend their practice so that they could work more effectively with pupils who present challenging behaviours. The ultimate test of treatment strategies which have evolved outside the school is whether they make sense to teachers and whether they can contribute to improved classroom practice in the medium and long term.

Summary

Among the main approaches to the challenging behaviours presented by adults and children with learning disabilities, interventions based on behavioural principles are by far the most frequently cited in the research literature. Recent developments in this field have emphasised the functional complexity of many challenging behaviours, the importance of multicomponent interventions, and the need to help people to develop positive and fulfilling lifestyles. The fundamental importance of human rights and the need to maintain the dignity and respect for those receiving treatment has been widely endorsed, although the extent to which aversive procedures may be justified in extreme circumstances remains subject to debate.

Concerns that behavioural methods inevitably lead to interventions which disregard the thoughts, feelings and motives of the children and adults who present challenging behaviour may also have affected the uptake of behavioural methods in schools. In contrast, there has been an enthusiastic response from clinicians and educators to therapeutic approaches which claim to be person-centred and to address challenging behaviours through the development of relationships and pro-social behaviours. While there is a great deal of interest in the methods described by Lovett, and McGee and his colleagues, it is too early to judge how they compare with more traditional behavioural approaches.

The choice between alternative methods for responding to challenging behaviours is closely tied to the question of effectiveness. While reductions in the frequency, duration or intensity of specific behaviours may be desirable, there are other equally important objectives, including increasing social interaction and participation in educational and extra-curricular activities. Judgments about efficacy must also be made in the light of the setting within which any approach will be employed. Interventions must not only have an impact on the child's behaviour, they must be practicable within the resource limitations of the school and, to the extent that teachers and care staff are directly involved, they should be seen as acceptable and worthwhile additions to the range of staff responsibilities.

Chapter 4

A SURVEY OF PUPILS WITH CHALLENGING
BEHAVIOUR IN SPECIAL SCHOOLS

At the start of the project, a screening questionnaire was designed to help in the selection of schools for the intervention study. It was divided into four sections: buildings and services covering topics such as overall numbers of pupils, age range, teaching and non-teaching staff, the number of classrooms and other resources; characteristics of pupils with challenging behaviour and approaches to management; school policy and views on participation in the project; support from other agencies.

An accompanying letter set out the criteria to be employed in judging whether or not a behaviour constituted a challenge (see Chapter 2). After asking about pupils with severe challenging behaviour, a further question invited comments on other pupils who could be described as presenting challenging behaviours. The questionnaire was kept deliberately brief in order to encourage prompt responses. A copy of the questionnaire and the accompanying letter to head teachers can be found in Appendix I.

The questionnaire was sent to head teachers of forty-four schools in the West Midlands, listed in the Educational Yearbook (1992) as making provision for pupils with severe learning difficulties. After two weeks, head teachers were contacted by telephone to check that they had received the questionnaire and to ask whether there were any problems in responding. Further telephone calls were made to head teachers who had not responded one month after the questionnaire was first sent.

Thirty-three completed questionnaires were returned giving a response of 75%. The schools ranged in size from 18 to 209 pupils with an average of 70. Schools making provision for pupils of all ages were larger (average of 79 pupils) than either primary schools (average 47) or secondary schools (average 55). Teacher pupil ratios ranged from 5:1 to 6.5:1 with an average of 6.3:1 .

Approximately 12% of students were identified as presenting a challenge to the schools as a result of their behaviour, and a further 15% were reported as presenting a severe problem arising from their challenging behaviours.

Schools which make provision for students from age three to nineteen and those which only cater for students aged eleven years and over reported a higher proportion of children with severe challenging behaviour compared to schools with only primary age students.

Table 4.1

The number of pupils identified as presenting challenging behaviours from postal questionnaire

Type of School	Number of Schools	Number of Pupils	Number of Pupils with Challenging Behaviour		Number of Pupils with Severely Challenging Behaviour	
				%		%
All age	23	1903	205	10.8	286	15.0
Primary	6	334	35	10.4	34	10.2
Secondary	4	220	27	12.3	33	15
TOTAL	33	2457	267		353	
			mean	10.9	mean	14.4

One all-age school (n = 107) and one primary school (n = 50) did not identify any pupils with challenging behaviour.

These figures support Kiernan and Kiernan's (1994) conclusion that, while there is a slight increase in the number of students described as presenting challenging behaviours with increasing age, there is a relatively large number of students who display challenging behaviour across the age range. Further research is needed to determine whether the increase in teacher identification of pupils presenting challenging behaviour with increased age reflects real changes in behaviour or can be attributed to increased teacher sensitivity towards difficult and inappropriate behaviour presented by older and physically more mature students.

Behaviours which challenge schools

After respondents had identified numbers of children with challenging behaviours and severe challenging behaviours, they were asked to describe the problems presented by these pupils. We then established a list of key words used in these behavioural descriptions. Table 4.2 provides a list of key words employed. A systematic search of all the descriptions of challenging and severely challenging behaviours determined how many responses included each of the key words. Two raters worked independently to locate key words and inter-rate r = rater reliability, calculated by dividing the total number of agreements by the number of agreements and disagreements, was found to be 84% for descriptions of challenging behaviours and 83% for descriptions of severe challenging behaviours. Where descriptions had been coded differently, discussion between the two raters established a consensus so that all the information was included in the data pool.

This procedure does not provide a detailed description of each behaviour presented by individual pupils. Instead it gives an indication of the kinds of behaviour which schools find challenging. The limitations of the questionnaire format, and time constraints, meant that it was not possible to establish how closely the respondents had adhered to the interpretative criteria set out in our letter, or to know whether certain criteria (for example, 'makes excessive demands on teachers') were more or less likely to be invoked when making judgments about behavioural challenges.

The behaviours listed in Table 4.2 are considered as 'challenging' within the context of the organisation, philosophy and practices of individual schools. They provide an indication of the behaviour management issues facing schools for children with severe learning difficulties, families, and all services working with this group of children.

Table 4.2
Challenging behaviours in schools

Frequency of behaviours identified as: (a) Challenging (b) Severely Challenging	Challenging Behaviours		Severely Challenging Behaviours	
Description of behaviour (keywords)	Number of Schools	Rank	Number of Schools	Rank
Physical aggression/attacks on others	13	1	24	1
Non-compliance/resistance to teaching or to contact with adults	12	2	7	5
Distracting/hyperactivity	10	3	9	3
Disruptive/interferes with work of the classroom	9	4	6	6
Lack of awareness of danger to self or others	3	5	5	7
Tantrums	3	5	2	9
Self-injurious behaviour	3	5	16	2
Shouting/swearing/increasing noise level	2	6	9	3
Damage to property/destruction	2	6	9	3
Running away	2	6	2	9
Verbal abuse	2	6	5	7
Isolation	1	7	0	0
Spitting	1	7	2	9
Throwing	1	7	1	10
Inappropriate sexual behaviour	1	7	3	8
Obsessional/ritualistic behaviour	0	0	8	4
Incontinence/soiling/smearing	0	0	3	8
Self-stimulation/sexual problems	0	0	2	9
Unpredictable behaviour	0	0	1	10

A wide range of behaviours was described and there is considerable overlap between the descriptions of challenging and severely challenging behaviours. Physical aggression, non-compliance, disruption and hyperactivity were the most frequently mentioned challenging behaviours. Physical aggression was also the most frequently identified severely challenging behaviour. Self-injurious behaviour, shouting and swearing and destruction of property were mentioned more often as severely challenging behaviours than as 'merely' challenging. Only four behaviours were identified by more than three schools as challenging, while ten behaviours were described by five or more schools as severely challenging. Obsessional or ritualistic behaviour, incontinence, soiling and smearing, self-stimulation, including masturbation, and unpredictability were all referred to exclusively as severely challenging behaviours.

Responding to students who present challenging behaviour

The main focus of the research project is to assist schools in their attempts to meet the needs of students who present challenging behaviours. In order to achieve this, it was important to discover how schools addressed the issue of challenging behaviours in formal policies and procedural guidelines, in the role of external agencies such as advisory teachers and psychologists, and in the range of strategies currently being employed. Respondents were asked to describe the school policy on the management of students presenting challenging behaviours, the strategies currently employed when responding to pupils with challenging behaviours and the support they received from outside agencies.

School policies on challenging behaviours

Of the schools who returned questionnaires, ten failed to provide either a policy document or a summary of current school policies. We analysed the information from the schools which did provide this information by identifying key words and searching through each policy document or summary to identify whether or not topics described by the key words were included. All the submitted materials were analysed by two raters working independently. Identification of key words in each response or policy document was compared across raters. Using the method of dividing total agreements by the sum of agreements and disagreements, overall reliability was found to be 75.4%. Disagreements were then resolved by discussion and included in the data pool.

The most frequently cited terms in the policy statements were concerned with community involvement and working with parents. Only six schools made any reference to behaviour or behaviour management. (Table 4.3).

A number of head teachers expressed their uncertainty and concern regarding the development of an appropriate policy framework and practical guidelines to assist staff in responding to pupils presenting challenging behaviours. In the words of one

Table 4.3

Frequency of key words in school policy statements
Total number of schools = 33

Statement of aims (keywords)	Number of Schools	Rank
Community involvement	14	1
Relationship with parents	13	2
Child focus	12	3
Social emotional development	10	4
Integration	10	4
Curriculum	9	5
Equal opportunities	6	6
Behaviour management	6	6
Expectations of staff	3	7
Care	3	7
Health and safety	3	7
Leisure skills	2	8
FE, TVEI and work preparation	2	8
Conservation and 'green' issues	2	8
School as centre of expertise	2	8
No statement provided	10	

head, 'We know what we can't do; what we don't know is what we *can* do'. This stands in sharp contrast to the recommendations made by McDonnell *et al* (1991) who suggest that policy statements on staff responses to challenging behaviour should include:

(i)   A clear definition of what is meant by challenging behaviour.
(ii)   Specific reference to strategies which can reduce the likelihood of challenging behaviours occurring.
(iii) Criteria for staff intervention in a violent situation.
(iv)   Recognition of appropriate training.
(v)   Procedures for recording incidents.
(vi)   List of support services available within and from outside the school.

Helping pupils with challenging behaviours

In case some schools had introduced strategies specifically to address the needs of pupils with challenging behaviours, but had not included them in the policy statements, we asked whether the school had adopted a general approach to the management of challenging behaviour. We also asked whether there were any guidelines or accepted strategies for responding to 'crisis situations'. Head teachers provided a variety of comments and, once again, we employed the 'key words' technique.

Reliability for two raters working independently was found to be 82.7% for descriptions of general approaches to the management of challenging behaviours and 71.2% for responses to crisis situations. Inconsistencies were subsequently resolved through discussion.

The majority of schools (21) referred to behaviour modification as the preferred method of dealing with challenging behaviours although none provided further elaboration of particular techniques or assessment strategies and only six schools referred to behaviour modification techniques in their policies on challenging behaviour. From the information provided, there was little to suggest that behavioural interventions were being systematically applied.

Table 4.4
General approaches to challenging behaviours

Total sample of schools = 33.

Policy Statements referred to	Number of Schools	Rank
Behaviour modification	21	1
Child focussed/individual approach	13	2
Gentle touching	7	3
Time out/seclusion/detention	6	4
Development/interactive approach	6	4
Reinforcement/praise	5	5
Eclectic approach	5	5
Understanding the behaviour	4	6
Positive approach	3	7
Distraction	3	7
Non-aversion/non-confrontational	3	7
Ignoring	2	8
Passive restraint	2	8
Therapeutic approach-massage/aromatherapy-relaxation techniques	2	8
Referral to the head teacher or to parents	2	8
Token economy system	1	9
Loss of privileges	1	9
Forced alternatives	1	9
Social skills teaching	1	9
Individual teaching	1	9
Referral to health services/medication	1	9
Integration	1	9

The second most popular approach was to emphasise the individuality of pupils with challenging behaviours and the importance of tailoring interventions to specific needs. Although we have included this information in the table, it is not clear whether it constitutes a recognisable approach or simply an orientation to pupils with challenging behaviours which might be more appropriately considered as part of a philosophy underlying all work with pupils with severe learning difficulties. Similarly, gentle teaching was referred to by seven schools without further elaboration and developmental or interactive approaches were mentioned by six schools. Aversive procedures such as time-out, seclusion and detention were mentioned by six schools.

Seven schools reported having written guidelines for dealing with crisis situations and provided complete documents or summaries. Other schools included a variety of *ad hoc* or very vague accounts of crisis intervention procedures: treat each situation individually; call a team meeting/case conference; avoid physical confrontation; use distraction; remove the pupil presenting challenging behaviours; time-out; restraint. (see Table 4.5).

On the evidence presented here, it is clear that most schools who responded to our questionnaire have only rudimentary policies and piecemeal practical guidelines on the most appropriate ways of responding to pupils with challenging behaviours. This is important because the absence of a well thought through and consistent

Table 4.5

Strategies for crisis management

Descriptions referred to	Number of Schools	Rank
Discussion among staff/meetings/mutual support/ communication of agreed strategies	15	1
Additional staff input - including head and deputy	13	2
Code of practice/guidelines/policy	11	3
Isolation of child - withdrawal/removal of others/ time out/exclusion	10	4
Consultation with professionals from outside school	8	5
Distraction/avoidance/minimal intervention/non-aversive approaches/gentle teaching	8	5
Restriction/restraint	6	· 6
Safety of pupils as first priority	6	6
Involvement of parents	6	6
Recording/observation/identification of contingencies	5	7

approach to challenging behaviours for the school as a whole will, inevitably, reduce the efficacy of any individual member of staff; children with significant and complex needs will receive less than optimum support; teachers are likely to experience frustration and stress because of the difficulties in deciding the scope and limits of their professional responsibilities to individual pupils.

Support from outside agencies

Schools were asked to indicate how frequently they received input from outside agencies. For medical and therapeutic services (physiotherapy, speech therapy), the majority of schools received visits on a weekly basis. However, for LEA support services such as advisors and advisory teachers and visits from educational psychologists, most schools reported only termly contact. Nearly 70% of schools were visited by clinical psychologists and social services less than once a term. We did not ask how much support these other professionals were able to provide specifically for teachers working with children who presented challenging behaviours or whether the contact was felt to be beneficial. However, the frequency of visits alone suggests that schools must rely predominantly on their own resources and expertise.

Table 4.6

Schools receiving help from other agencies
Total number of schools = 33

Agency	Daily	Weekly	Half Termly	Termly	Less than Termly or none
LEA support services	0	4	12	7	10
Educational Psychologists	0	5	20	5	3
Clinical Psychologists	0	2	3	4	24
Physiotherapy	11	19	0	0	3
Speech therapy	4	27	0	0	2
School's medical officer	1	13	13	0	6
Social Services	0	6	2	2	23
Other (OT, music and therapy, visual and hearing impaired)	2	14	4	2	11

Preparation of staff for working with pupils who present challenging behaviour

It is widely recognised that working with adults and children who have learning disabilities and challenging behaviour requires special expertise (Kiernan & Bliss, 1994; Cornick & Cornick, 1994). In order to work effectively with pupils with challenging behaviours, teachers will require a wide range of skills, some of which will lie outside the range of competencies usually associated with education. Indeed, the development of effective ways of working with these and other pupils with complex needs emphasises the multiple roles which teachers are expected to fulfil.

We asked the head teachers completing our questionnaire whether they had made any arrangements for preparing staff to respond to challenging behaviours. The responses are summarised in Table 4.7.

Table 4.7

Staff Training

Type of training	Number of Schools	Rank
Staff meetings/sharing information	15	1
School-based courses	9	2
LEA courses organised by:		
(a) Learning support services	7	3
(b) Educational Psychology Service	5	5
Other courses:		
(a) EDY	6	4
(b) Passive Restraint	6	4
(c) Behavioural techniques other than EDY	4	6
(d) Clinical Psychology input	3	7
(e) Other	6	4
(f) Training for non-teaching staff	2	8

For most schools (15) staff development for working with pupils with challenging behaviours was accomplished through staff meetings and other school-based courses. Less than a quarter of the schools which responded had arranged for staff to participate in courses run by the LEA support services, or educational psychologists. Six schools referred to courses on the Education of the Developmentally Young (EDY: Foxen and McBrien, 1981) organised by Manchester University, and training on passive restraint, offered by staff in the School of Psychology at the University of Birmingham, was also mentioned by six schools. Unfortunately, in the screening questionnaire, we were unable to explore the numbers of teachers involved in each school, why more schools had not participated in training courses and to what extent the courses referred to here provided staff with useful skills.

The small number of schools which had arranged for staff training on challenging behaviour is particularly worrying in view of the very limited support available from professionals outside the school (see Table 4.6). It seems unlikely that teachers will be able to address the social and educational needs of a significant number of pupils who present severely challenging behaviours without additional advice and in-service training.

Summary

In most schools for children with severe difficulties, as many as 25% of the pupils are regarded as presenting a challenge to the staff because of their behaviour and, of these, about 15% are regarded as presenting a severe challenge. While schools are clearly aware of the complex needs of these pupils and the impact they have on their peers, staff and school organisation, we found little evidence of clearly articulated intervention strategies being introduced. This is, perhaps, not surprising. For the past five years most schools have been fully occupied in trying to keep pace with the introduction of the National Curriculum. Furthermore, there has been little leadership from either the Department for Education or local education authorities regarding the introduction of school policies on challenging behaviours or how schools might most effectively respond to those pupils whose behaviour presents a challenge. The data presented in this chapter indicates that teachers have very little support from professionals outside the school and few opportunities to attend training courses on the topic.

Chapter 5

WORKING IN SCHOOLS

'More than anything else, effective strategies for implementation require an under-standing of the process, a way of thinking that cannot be captured by any list of steps or phases to be followed.' (Fullan, 1991, p.65)

In this chapter, we describe the nature of the consultancy support made available to the schools. This is based upon the concept of intervention as a process which engages all members of staff and may require change and innovation in many different areas. Following a brief description of the schools who participated in the study, we review the whole school meetings and the selection of pupils. In the remainder of the chapter we look at the way in which specific challenging behaviours were identified and the approaches to intervention developed by staff in collaboration with the project team.

A whole school approach

Throughout this chapter we emphasise the development of a process by which schools can begin to understand and respond to pupils who present a challenge. We have used the term 'process' for a number of reasons:

- First, the approach we adopted required participation from the whole school and not only the particular members of staff who are currently responsible for pupils presenting a challenge.

- Secondly, we wanted staff to reflect upon their attitudes and work practices in respect of pupils who challenge. This could involve rethinking how they worked with individual pupils or it might require a more fundamental reappraisal of their approach to challenging behaviour in general.

- Thirdly, to develop new ways of working with pupils who present a challenge, schools would need to embrace many different kinds of change; possibly includ-ing the use of new materials, the development of new styles of interaction, working differently with colleagues or modifying organisational systems.

- Fourthly, the goal of working more effectively with pupils who challenge does not have an easily recognisable end product. There will always be pupils with severe learning disabilities who present challenging behaviours and some pupils will continue to challenge over long periods of time. A 'process approach' indicates how schools can respond positively to pupils who challenge without implying that there are fixed-term 'treatments' which solve the problem and eradicate the challenge once and for all.

- Fifthly, we felt that if schools were to respond positively, our approach should be minimally disruptive of existing educational practice and sufficiently flexible to accommodate differences between schools. The project team did not set out to introduce predetermined interventions strategies, but to help staff to develop methods which would work within their own school. Innovations would need to be compatible with established educational priorities, existing resources and current classroom practice. The objective was not to impose innovation but to establish a process which could lead to innovation.

- Finally, the approach we adopted was based upon continuous collaboration between the project team and the school staff. At the start of the project we initiated contact with schools and proposed a procedure for introducing the change process. This involved a series of meetings described below. Once agreed, the meetings between the project team and various members of the schools staff provided a structure within which the intervention process could flourish.

The schools

The schools which participated in the project are, in many respects, indistinguishable from many other schools that serve pupils with severe learning disabilities (see Table 5:1). Three were all-age schools with pupils as young as 3 and as old as 19. Two were predominantly for pupils at primary school age, three made provision only for pupils over the age of 11 and one took pupils between 7 and 19. The largest school is a local authority day school with 107 pupils while the smallest, also an LEA day school, had only thirty pupils. The average number of pupils in all nine schools was 61.

Three schools had on-site residential provision. One had a twelve bedded unit attached which was not being used at the time of the project. Another had developed a reputation for working with pupils who have complex needs and communication problems and used the residential complex to accommodate pupils on 'out of area' placements. The third was an independent residential school located in a rural area where the majority of the pupils are on 'out of area' placements.

All nine schools were well staffed with the ratio of teaching staff to pupils ranging from as high as 1:4 to as low as 1:7. None of the schools were located in ideal buildings and two lacked any special purpose-built facilities. The amount of space in and around the school varied according to the geographical location. Three of the schools located in inner city areas were formally junior training centres. They had the least amount of space, and staff operated in relatively cramped conditions;

Table 5:1

Summary of the Project Schools

Phase I Schools					Phase II Schools					
School	No. of Pupils	Ages	Teaching staff/ pupil ratio	Non-teaching staff/ pupil ratio	Buildings	School	No. of pupils	Ages	Teaching staff/ pupil ratio	Non-teaching staff/ pupil ratio	Buildings
Merry School	46	3-19	1:5	1:4	Modern, large classrooms, grassed play areas	Joyful School	44	11-19	1:4	1:4	Former JTC. Teaching and space severely limited
Bright School	47	5-19	1:6	1:5	Former JTC. Limited classroom and tarmacked play space	Lively School	40	3-13	1:5.5	1:5.5	Large, modern, spacious buildings includes residential unit for 12 pupils
Pleasant School	107	3-19	1:7	1:7	Modern, spacious Extensive grassed play areas	Jolly School	105	7-19	1:4.5	1:5	Modern, spacious school buildings attached to large residential home. Set in extensive site in open countryside
Friendly School	54	11-19	1:7.5	1:7	Former JTC. Limited classroom space and tarmacked play space	Cheerful School	30	11-19	1:4.5	1:4	Large, spacious purpose-built teaching areas and residential accommodation. Extensive site with fields and trees
Happy School	76	3-13	1:5.5	1:6	Modern building; spacious, open teaching spaces; grassed outdoor play areas.						

those in suburban areas were more modern, enjoyed better facilities in general, had bigger classrooms and access to large areas of enclosed space around the school.

Whole school meetings

We felt it was important that, right from the start, all staff were aware of the project and understood the reasons for our emphasis on a whole school approach. For this reason, following our initial contacts with the head teacher, we asked for a meeting with all members of the school staff. In those schools with residential places, care staff also attended. The following topics were addressed.

Collaboration: We introduced the project team and explained the aims and objectives of the project. We indicated why we felt it was important to work in partnership with teachers and how this could be accomplished. It was emphasised that, throughout the project, responsibility for pupils who presented a challenge would remain with the teachers, and classroom support workers.

Effectiveness: We wanted members of the school staff to be clear at the outset what we felt were realistic outcomes for pupils who presented challenging behaviours. While a reduction in the occurrence of challenging behaviours might be desirable, it was not always possible. Reducing the disruptive consequences of challenging behaviours, without necessarily changing the behaviour, could also be a positive outcome. Similarly, increasing the level of participation in ordinary (special) school activities by pupils with challenging behaviours, should be seen as progress, even though the problematic behaviour might not have changed.

The school setting: An important goal was the development of methods of working with pupils which could be integrated within the school setting. For example:

- existing routines and practices;

- the needs of other pupils;

- established educational aims and objectives;

- the expertise and experience of the staff

were all acknowledged as aspects of school activity which had to be considered when developing specific interventions.

From the point of view of the project staff, it was intended that collaboration would have two specific outcomes:

Staff ownership: First, by involving staff in developing, implementing, and monitoring methods of working with pupils who challenge, we hoped to establish a body of expertise within the school which would be self sustaining after the project was completed. Ideally, schools would assimilate the process model and use it to develop strategies for working with others pupils who presented a challenge.

Transferable expertise: Secondly, we wanted to use the project schools to test out the process model in order that it could be modified and adapted. At the end of the project, we hoped to use the accumulated experience of the nine project schools to prepare workshop training materials which could be used by staff in other schools.

Selection of pupils

At the end of the first whole-school meeting staff were asked to select pupils who could be directly involved in the study. The main criterion for selection was that they should display behaviour which was likely to have one or more of the following consequences:

- Prevents participation in educational activities

- Isolates pupils from their peers

- Affects the learning of other pupils

- Drastically reduces opportunities for involvement in ordinary community activities

- Makes excessive demands on staff and other resources

- Places the child or other pupils in physical danger

- Threatens the prospects of future placement.

In addition, the schools were asked to obtain parental approval for specific interventions to address challenging behaviour and to ensure that the classroom staff responsible for the selected pupils were able to commit time and energy to working alongside the project team. It was suggested that each school selected between two and three pupils for inclusion in the project.

Challenges presented by the pupils

The various ways in which each of the 24 pupils presented a challenge are set out in summary form by school. The names of the pupils and the schools have been changed to protect confidentiality. Raw scores from the Vineland Adaptive Behaviour Scales are presented in Table 5.2.

Phase I schools

Friendly school

Charles (aged 17) has aggressive outbursts directed towards staff and other pupils which often last as long as an hour. Charles appears distressed and disorientated during these episodes.

Mary (aged 15) behaves aggressively towards staff and other pupils. She causes general disruption by running around the classroom and by shouting and screaming.

Cliff (aged 13) often refuses to respond when asked to do something. He pinches staff and other pupils and occasionally becomes more generally aggressive.

Table 5:2
Pupils participating in the study: Ages and Raw Vineland Scores

School	Pupil	Age - years+ months	Commn	Std. Score	Daily Living	Std. Score	Social	Std. Score	Motor Skills	Est. Std. Score	Maladap Part 1	Maladap Part 2
Friendly	Charles	17.0	56	-	113	37	54	-	71	108	15	20
	Mary	15.4	46	-	65	-	52	20	52	51	37	45
	Cliff	13.9	31	-	78	-	52	32	46	47	23	23
Bright	Carol	7.5	28	36	39	22	30	48	44	45	22	33
	Colin	8.11	22	27	44	-	20	36	45	46	28	38
	Harry	14.5	49	-	69	-	55	-	49	49	27	34
Happy	Stephen	13.3	19	-	37	-	22	-	43	44	38	54
	Angela	11.7	23	-	30	-	27	24	44	45	23	30
	Ben	11.3	4	-	11	-	10	-	9	-	27	36
Merry	*Tony											
	Alan	8.8	19	27	27	-	32	45	45	46	33	43
	Robert	18.8	17	-	87	-	53	-	64	78	36	47
Pleasant	*Heather											
	John	13.0	29	-	43	-	28	-	559	65	20	28
	Nigel	7.0	20	34	51	37	33	50	59	65	16	23
Joyful	Michael	18.2	63	-	97	-	50	-	51	65	25	33
	Martin	15.6	27	-	30	-	26	-	27	27	15	18
	Simon	16	27	-	14	-	23	-	31	31	20	24
Lively	Jack	7.2	46	44	60	45	56	60	53	52	22	28
	Mick	6.0	36	46	49	48	39	40	61	70	29	40
	Neil	7.5	48	44	57	39	46	53	47	47	20	20
Jolly	Adam	13.3	13	-	16	-	16	-	32	33	29	36
	Ruth	16.0	21	-	41	-	19	-	61	70	8*	38
	Darren	9.10	18	22	31	-	19	28	48	48	19	26
Cheerful	Chris	11.11	30	-	31	-	21	20	53	52	33	44
	Clive	16.8	54	-	80	-	36	-	67	87	30	38

Notes:
1. Standard scores have a mean of 100 and a standard deviation of 15.
2. The conversion tables do not provide standard scores below 20. On this page standard scores of below 20 are shown with a dash (-).
3. Standard scores for motor skills are estimates based on the norms for children below 6 years of age.
4. Maladaptive behaviour scores Part 1 are rated 'non-significant', 'intermediate' or 'significant'. All the scores shown in this table are rated 'significant' except for the score obtained by Ruth (*) which is rated 'intermediate'.
   *Tony is at a very early developmental stage and it was not considered appropriate to administer the Vineland.
   *Heather experienced frequent absences from school and was withdrawn from participation in the study.

Bright school

Carol (aged 7) is aggressive towards other pupils and staff. She screams and frequently throws equipment or deliberately destroys things. She avoids interacting with staff by throwing herself on the floor.

Colin (aged 9) runs around the classroom and is always picking up and eating non-food items. He pinches and bites other pupils, targeting one pupil in particular.

Harry (aged 14) is generally noisy and disruptive. He hits other pupils and seems to be deliberately unco-operative. Occasionally, he behaves in very odd ways, for example, by dropping to the ground and refusing to move, especially when on trips out of school.

Happy school

Stephen (aged 13) pinches and bites staff and other pupils. He repeatedly slaps his mouth, thighs and abdomen. He engages in frequent anal fingering, hand flicking, eating non-food items, bizarre staring and repetitive singing. He seems unable to concentrate for more than a few seconds at a time and is completely lacking communication skills.

Angela (aged 11) grabs materials at random but quickly loses interest in them. She constantly moves about the classroom, often taking off her shoes and socks and sometimes her clothes. She is always looking for food and seems to be obsessed with water. She is aggressive towards other pupils when not closely supervised, for example, at break times. She seems unable to occupy herself for even a short time and staff find her difficult to motivate.

Ben (aged 11) screams and thrashes around, often for as long as two or three hours at a time. He grabs and bites other pupils and often bites his own hands. He regularly regurgitates food.

Merry school

Tony (aged 4) seems to have very little self control when moving around; he knocks things over, rips up pictures. Consequently, he is often restrained. He chews his clothing, masturbates and rubs or slaps his head and ears.

Alan (aged 9) frequently and repeatedly slaps his head causing redness and bruising. He screams and shouts for most of the day unless physically restrained by staff.

Robert (aged 18) displays temper tantrums during which he lies on the floor, hits himself and anyone else who gets in the way, bites his clothing and furniture. After the tantrums, which often last between one and two hours, he seems distressed. He talks to himself, often very aggressively, with lots of swearing and sometimes seems to be talking to the palm of his hand.

Pleasant school

Heather (aged 12) always seems unhappy and unresponsive. She is difficult to engage in activities and she avoids all forms of social contact. Most of the time she runs around or jumps up and down. Occasionally, she has prolonged bouts of loud screaming. She is aggressive towards other pupils, often picking on one particular child.

John (aged 13) continually moves around the classroom and, whenever an opportunity occurs, he runs out of the classroom and out of the school. He is unco-operative and, when not supervised, he destroys or damages equipment and materials by throwing, kicking and tearing. He occasionally tries to grab and scratch staff.

Nigel (aged 7) is unable to concentrate for more than a few seconds and spends most of his time aimlessly running around the classroom. If unsupervised, he turns water taps full on and plays with the water.

Phase II schools

Joyful school

Martin (aged 15) is aggressive, often pulling hair or clothes or throwing objects at people. Although capable of walking, he avoids participating in activities by sliding off his chair and shuffling around on his bottom.

Michael (aged 18) constantly displays verbal aggression, during which he shouts, makes loud non-speech noises, jabs his forefinger, bangs the table, door or wall. He is unco-operative and often responds to requests by becoming verbally aggressive, covering his face with his hands and turning away. At other times, he displays inappropriate and over enthusiastic greeting behaviour. He is often reluctant to pass through doorways into rooms.

Simon (aged 16) spends much of his time crying and being unco-operative. He often refuses to walk and pushes people and materials away. At mealtimes, he refuses to eat, pushing food away and throwing drinks on the floor.

Lively school

Jack (aged 7) is difficult to engage in activities. He slaps the table, taps his feet, moves his chair away from the table, shouts and makes noises, sits on the floor, moves away from the group, pinches and slaps other pupils, rubs his forehead and sucks his thumb.

Mick (aged 6) frequently grabs and scratches other pupils, often picking on those who are most vulnerable. He refuses to join in class activities and disrupts other pupils by shouting and crying.

Neil (aged 7) is unco-operative. He fiddles with things, whines, screams and shouts and, if not closely supervised, will run out of the classroom. He fails to respond to simple requests and often interferes with other pupils.

Jolly school

Adam (aged 13) bites and scratches staff and other pupils, rips down wall displays and destroys equipment. He screams a lot and regurgitates food. He has two disruptive stereotypic behaviours which occur continuosly unless he is physically restrained; he avoids eye contact by moving his head rhythmically from side to side and he constantly strokes his hands together 'as if counting money'.

Ruth (aged 16) bites and pinches herself, staff and other pupils. If not physically prevented, she constantly runs around the classroom, twirling in circles and flicking either her hands and fingers or materials such as paper, dusters or tea towels. At the same time, she cries or moans. She makes frequent and apparently unnecessary visits to the toilet.

Darren (aged 9) likes to climb on to the high classroom window sills where he will sit quietly gazing out. He taps his hands or fingers constantly in a ritualistic manner. He seems obsessed with water and other liquids, often drinking paint or playing with spittle. Sometimes he has screaming tantrums during which he bites other people.

Cheerful school

Chris (aged 12) throws things and pinches himself and other people. He spits on his hands and wipes them on other people. He frequently drops to his knees while walking and will lick the floor, walls, furniture or the toilet seat. All these behaviours occur more frequently when he is asked to do things and before particular activities. They are often preceded by giggling.

Clive (aged 16) constantly flaps his hands in front of his face and around his groin making loud noises, screaming, stamping his feet and banging doors, tables and walls. He sometimes grabs staff and sinks his nails into their hands. He regularly twirls around rapidly while standing in one place.

Once pupils had been selected, the project team worked with staff to collect and summarise additional information about the nature of the challenge they presented. A number of data collection methods were employed:

- Teachers in Phase I schools participated in a semi-structured interview (see Appendix 1).

- For teachers in Phase II schools, the interview was replaced by a shorter and more concise self-report questionnaire (see Appendix 1).

- The project staff undertook classroom observations in which they 'shadowed' one of the selected pupils and made detailed notes.

- Teachers were asked to make systematic recordings of challenging behaviours using pre-prepared record sheets (see Appendix 1).

- Vineland Adaptive Behaviour Scales (survey version) were completed with the class teacher as the primary informant (see Table 5:2).

In the second part of this chapter we include information provided by teachers during the interviews and when completing the questionnaire. In Chapter 6 we provide a detailed account of the Review Meetings and the interventions which were proposed for each of the pupils selected for involvement in the study. Initially interviews were carried out with teachers in Phase I schools and self-report questionnaires were completed by teachers in Phase II schools.

The semi-structured interview and the self-report questionnaire were used both to facilitate the process of teacher-researcher collaboration and to provide a method of collecting factual information about pupils with problem behaviours and the way in which their needs were currently being addressed within schools. Where a Phase I teacher was responsible for more than one pupil selected for the study, the interview was repeated. Phase II teachers with responsibility for more than one pupil in the study were asked to complete additional questionnaires. In this section information is presented in relation to the following questions:

- What types of behaviour were perceived by teachers as challenging?

- With what frequency did the behaviours occur and how severe were they judged to be?

- What were the social and educational consequences which contributed to these behaviours being judged 'challenging'?

- How did staff typically respond to such behaviours?

What behaviours were regarded as challenging?
Inevitably, teachers described a wide variety of behaviours which they perceived as raising special problems. In Tables 5:3 and 5:4 they are itemised for pupils in Phase I and Phase II schools separately, as a different research instrument was employed.

Classifying these disparate behaviours is not easy. The 'free response' format for both the interview and the questionnaire resulted in different types of description ranging from those focusing on topography (turns on taps; takes shoes off; runs in classroom) to those which imply some form of interpretative criteria (aggression; distractibility). Furthermore, it is clear that for any set of interpretative criteria employed, some behaviours might easily fit into two or more categories. Thirdly, there is an important distinction between behaviours categorised on the basis of perceived intention (attention seeking; avoidance of eye contact) and those which are described in terms of their outcome (disruption; non-compliance).

While there is no completely satisfactory solution to this problem, it was considered helpful to provide some form of summary classification. The following headings have been used:

Aggression (A) refers to any behaviour which is likely to cause harm or inflicts pain on another person.

Inappropriate Noises (IN) refers to screaming, shouting, swearing and inappropriate vocalisations.

Misuse of Property (P) refers to behaviour which damages materials or risks inadvertent damage to materials, for example, throwing, chewing clothes.

Disruption (DIS) refers to behaviour which is likely to adversely affect other pupils in the classroom or requires the intervention of the teacher. It includes chair rocking, banging furniture and grabbing objects/materials. Some teachers simply referred to 'disruption'.

Socially Inappropriate Behaviour (SI) refers to actions which may interfere with a pupil's participation in classroom activities or be considered unacceptable for other reasons. It includes hand flicking, playing with food and undressing.

Non-compliance (NC) refers to behaviours which result in the pupil removing himself or herself from activities, for example, getting up 'out of seat' or falling to the floor as well as 'refusals' to co-operate.

Self-injury and Self-stimulation (SS) refer to any behaviours which produce repeated physical contact between parts of the pupil's body, including masturbation. Note that here, hand flapping and hand waving are classified as socially inappropriate behaviours.

Distractibility (DIST) was a term used by a number of teachers without elaboration and may encompass a number of quite different behaviours. It is included here as a separate category although it has an obvious overlap with non-compliance and socially inappropriate behaviours.

Regurgitation (REG) and **Pica (PIC)** are relatively specific behaviours which do not require further clarification.

Table 5.3
Behaviours described as challenging and teacher ratings of frequency and severity
Phase 1 schools; based on semi-structured interviews
Severity: 1 = least severe and 5 = most severe

School/ Pupil	Behaviour	Frequency	Severity Rating
Friendly			
Charles	Aggression (A)	daily	4-5
Mary*	Aggression (A)	daily	5
	Running in classroom (R)	daily	4
	Shouting and screaming (IN)	daily	4
Cliff	Non-compliance (NC)	daily	2
	Pinching others (A)	daily	3
	Aggression (A)	<weekly	4
Bright			
Carol*	Biting/scratching (A)	>weekly	4
	Screams (IN)	>weekly	4
	Throws equipment (P)	>weekly	4
	Throws self on floor (NC)	>weekly	4
Colin*	Running in class (R)	>weekly	3
	Biting and pinching (A)	>weekly	5
	Eats 'everything' (PIC)	<weekly	4
Harry*	Aggression (A)	daily-<weekly	3
	Inappropriate noises (IN)	daily-<weekly	4-5
	'Disruption' (DIS)	daily-<weekly	5
	'Bizarre' behaviour (SI)	daily-<weekly	5
Happy			
Stephen*	Pinches (A)	daily	4
	Bites (A)	<weekly	4
	Self-stimulation (SS)	hourly	5
	Hand-flicking (SI)	hourly (constant)	2
	Pica (PIC)	hourly (constant)	3
	Staring (SI)	hourly	2-3
	Distractibilty (DIST)	hourly (constant)	3-4
	Inappropriate noises (IN)	hourly (constant)	3
Angela	Grabbing things (DIS)	hourly (constant)	5
	Playing with food (SI)	hourly (constant)	3
	'Out of seat' (NC)	hourly	5
	Playing with water (SI)	hourly-<daily	3-4
	Aggression to peers (A)	playtimes	5
	Taking shoes off (SI)	hourly (constant)	2
	Undressing (SI)	weekly	1
	Distractibility (DIST)	hourly (constant)	5
Ben	Shouts and screams (IN)	daily (long periods)	4-5
	Waves arms (SI)	daily	3-4
	Grabs and bites peers (A)	>daily	5
	Bites own hands (SS)	daily	4-5
	Regurgitates food (REG)	daily	4-5

Table 5.3 - continued

School/ Pupil	Behaviour	Frequency	Severity Rating
Merry			
Tony*	Purposeless activity (SI)	hourly (constant)	1
	Disruption (DIS)	hourly (constant)	3
	Sucking and chewing clothes (P)	daily	2
	Masturbation/self stimulation (SS)	daily (depends on clothing)	4
	Rubbing and slapping head (SS)	daily	5
Alan*	Slapping face and head (SS)	hourly (constant)	4-5
	Shouting and crying (NI)	hourly	4-5
Robert	Tantrums (lies on floor, hits self and others, bites clothing and furniture) (NC)	daily	5
	Swearing and talking to self (IN)	daily	3
Pleasant			
Heather	Socially unresponsive (SI)	daily	2
	Aggression to peers (A)	daily	3
	Running in classroom (R)	>weekly	3
	Screaming (N)	>weekly	2
John	Running in and out of classroom (R)	hourly (constant)	4-5
	Distractibility (DIST)	hourly (constant)	4-5
	Destruction of property (P)	<weekly	4-5
	Aggression to staff (A)	<weekly	4-5
Nigel*	Turns tap on (SI)	hourly	1
	Running away (R)	hourly	1
	Distractibility (DIST)	hourly (x6)	2
	Non-compliance (NC)	daily	3
	'Obsessions' (SI)	hourly (x5)	3

* Indicates pupils who were involved in intervention study

Table 5.4
Behaviours described as challenging and teacher ratings of frequency and severity
Phase II Schools based on self-report questionnaires

Disruption: 1 = least disruptive
                5 = most disruptive

Risk of injury: 1 = no risk of injury to N or others
                2 = risk of minor injury to N or others
                3 = minor injury occurs or is likely to occur
                4 = risk of serious injury
                5 = serious injury occurs or is likely to occur

Rank: Teacher rating of degree of challenge
                1 = most challenging behaviour

School/Pupil	Behaviour	Frequency	Disruption	Risk of injury	Rank
Joyful					
Martin	Pulling hair (A)	daily	2	1	3
	Grabbing clothes (A)	hourly	1	1	2
	Throwing clothing (P)	hourly	2	2	1
	Sliding off chair (NC)	hourly	1-2	1	-
Michael	Verbal aggression/ inappropriate noises (IN)	daily	2	1	1
	Non-compliance (NC)	daily	2	1	2
	Requires prompting to enter rooms (SI)	daily	1	1	-
	Inappropriate greeting behaviour (SI)	daily	1	1	3
Simon	Crying 'without reason' (IN)	daily	4	1	1
	Refusing to walk (NC)	daily	1	1	2
	Refusing to eat (NC)	weekly	1	1	-
	Throwing drinks (P)	weekly	2	2	-
	Pushing people and things away (NC)	daily	2	2	3
Lively					
Jack	Blowing raspberries (IN)	hourly	5	1	-
	Rocking in chair (DIS)	hourly	5	1	-
	Banging hands and feet (DIST)	hourly	5	1	-
	Laughing inappropriately (IN)	hourly	5	1	-
	Attention seeking (SI)	hourly	5	1	-
Mick	Scratching (A)	hourly	5	4	1
	Picking plaster from walls (P)	hourly	1	1	-
	Pushing peers (A)	-	-	-	-
	Running around room (R)	-	-	-	3
Neil	Fiddles with objects (SI)	hourly	3	1	-
	Runs out of classroom (R)	hourly	3	2	1
	Whining/shouting/crying noises (IN)	hourly	3	1	2
	Distractibility (DIST)	hourly	3	1	3
	Annoying other pupils (DIS)	hourly	3	1	-

Table 5.4 continued

School/Pupil	Behaviour	Frequency	Disruption	Risk of Injury	Rank
Jolly					
Adam	Avoiding eye contact and head-waving (SI)	hourly	3	1	1
	Stereotypic hand movements (SI)	hourly	3	1	2
	Biting and scratching others (A)	daily	3	4	3
	Screaming (IN)	daily	3	1	-
	Regurgitates food (REG)	daily	3	1	-
	Pulls down wall displays (P)	-	-	-	-
Ruth	Pinching adults (A)	daily	5	3	1
	Kicking adults (A)	daily	5	3	-
	Visits to toilet (SI)	hourly	1	1	2
	Throwing objects (P)	weekly	4	3	3
Darren	Obsessive water play (SL)	hourly	2	2	1
	Climbing on cupboards and window sills (SI)	hourly	1	4	2
	Hand tapping (SI)	hourly	1	1	-
	Screaming (IN)	weekly	5	2	3
	Bites others (A)	-	-	-	-
Cheerful					
Chris	Throwing things (P)	daily	2	3	2
	Dropping on to knees (NC)	hourly	1	2	-
	Spitting on hand/playing with spit (SI)	daily	2	1	-
	Kicking floor and furniture (DIST)	hourly	1	3	3
	Pinching self and others (SS/A)	daily	2	5	1
Clive	Hand flapping (SI)	hourly	3	1	3
	Hand flapping ingroin (SI)	hourly	3	1	-
	Screaming (IN)	hourly	5	1	2
	Digs nails in people (A)	daily	5	5	1
	Stamping and banging (DIST)	hourly	2	1	-
	'Twirls' (SI)	daily	2	1	-

In Phase I, teachers rated behaviours in respect of severity. In Phase II, they rated behaviours in terms of disruption. In Table 5.5 the mean values for severity and disruption ratings are shown for each group of behaviours, together with the number of behaviours for which a rating was provided in brackets.

Table 5.5

Summary of behaviours described by teachers as challenging

Aggression 23 (1 not rated)
Mean severity 4.07 (N = 13); Mean disruption 3.2 (N = 9)   Combined 3.7

Socially Inappropriate Behaviours 25 (1 not rated)
Mean severity 2.3 (N = 12); Mean disruption 2.15 (N = 13)   Combined 2.24

Inappropriate Noises 16
Mean severity 3.5 (N = 8); Mean disruption 4.12 (N = 8)   Combined 3.8

Non Compliance 11
Mean severity 3.8 (N = 5); Mean disruption 1.3 (N = 6)   Combined 2.45

Misuse of Property 9
Mean severity 3.3 (N = 3); Mean disruption 2.3 (N = 6)   Combined 2.67

Disruption 9
Mean severity 4.0 (N = 4); Mean disruption 3.2 (N = 5)   Combined 3.5

Running 7 (1 not rated)
Mean severity 3.0 (N = 5); Mean disruption N/A   Combined 3.0

Self-lnjury/stimulation 6
Mean severity 4.4 (N = 5); Mean disruption N/A   Combined 4.0

Distractibility 5
Mean severity 3.5 (N = 4); Mean disruption N/A   Combined 3.4

Regurgitation 2
Means combined 3.5

Pica 2
Means combined 3.5

The most frequently mentioned behaviours are grouped under the following headings:

> Aggression (23)
> Socially inappropriate behaviour (25)
> Inappropriate noises (16)
> Non-compliance (11)

The behaviours noted as posing the most serious challenge by teachers in Phase II were:

> Throwing objects (P)
> Inappropriate noises (IN)

Crying 'without reason' (IN)
Whining, shouting, crying (IN)
Scratching (A)
Avoiding eye contact and hand waving (Sl)
Pinching adults (A)
Obsessive water play (Sl)
Pinching self and others (A/SS)
Digging nails in people (A)

Of these, four were classed as aggression, three as inappropriate noises, and two as socially inappropriate behaviours.

From Table 5.5 it can be seen that aggression, inappropriate noises, non-compliance, self injury/self stimulation, disruption and distractibility, are rated high in terms of severity. Socially inappropriate behaviours are rated low in terms of severity. In terms of the 'disruption' rating, inappropriate noises are rated most highly, with aggression ranking second along with behaviours described as 'disruptive'. Non-compliance, and socially inappropriate behaviours are rated low on this scale. This suggests that these two measures may be relatively independent of each other and that interventions may be most usefully directed at behaviours which are rated highly disruptive rather than those that are 'severe'. This is consistent with the philosophy underlying the increasing use of the term 'challenging behaviour'.

Secondly, the table indicates that many behaviours which are initially identified as presenting a challenge are not rated highly on either 'severity' or 'disruption'. This suggests that they are perceived as a challenge for other reasons, for example, they may be irritating to adults or inappropriate to the pupil's age. Many behaviours identified as 'socially inappropriate' fall into this category and further work is required to determine whether they were identified in respect of one or more of the criteria presented by the research team, or for other reasons. Evidence from the classroom-based work with teachers described in the next chapter suggests that at least some of the teachers were identifying behaviours which were atypical, without giving careful consideration to whether or not the social and educational consequences of the behaviours justified intensive interventions.

What were the social and educational consequences of behaviours judged as challenging?

During the semi-structured interview, after describing behaviours which were perceived as presenting problems for staff, teachers were asked 'In what ways does the child's behaviour create problems for himself/herself?' and 'How does the child's behaviour create problems for other children?' The self-report questionnaire asked the same two questions but provided multiple choice options as well as an open 'other' category.

Table 5.6
Problems for pupils with challenging behaviour

Type of problem	Phase I N = 11	Phase II N = 11
Isolation from peers	5	8
Access to the curriculum	5	8
Access to extra curricula activities	5	7
Risk of injury to self or others	4	7

All three items were included as response options in the questionnaire.

Teachers who were interviewed also mentioned reduced interaction with the environment (1), distress for the pupil (6) and reduced personal freedom, presumably because of management strategies, (1). One respondent to the questionnaire indicated that problem behaviour leads to staff losing patience. It is interesting that personal distress for the pupil concerned is not mentioned in the most widely used interpretative criteria for determining what constitutes a challenge (Emerson *et al*, 1987; Zarkowska and Clements, 1988); and yet six out of eleven staff spontaneously mentioned this at interview.

Table 5.7
Problems for other pupils

Type of problem	Phase I N = 11	Phase II N = 11
Disruption of teaching	9	10
Disruption of play/leisure	4	5
Injury or risk of injury	7	5

All four items were included as response options in the questionnaire.
Each respondent could endorse more than one category.

At interview, four respondents referred to the pupil 'taking the teacher's attention' which may be another way of describing disruption to teaching. Two teachers referred to other pupils being frightened and two to destruction of property. One teacher said that her response to the pupil concerned frightened other pupils.

Isolation, risk of injury, access to curricular and other activities and personal distress are perceived as potential consequences for the pupils who present difficult behaviours, but no single outcome stands out from the others. However, the pattern of responses to questions about consequences for other pupils is rather different, with over 80% identifying disruption of teaching as an adverse outcome.

These results underline the importance of the social context within which judgments about challenging behaviours are made. In the classroom, the teacher's commitment to 'providing education' establishes a framework of practices and expectations. Pupil behaviour which is perceived as being incompatible with the achievement of educational objectives is likely to be regarded as presenting a challenge. At present, relatively little is known about the interaction between formal curriculum guidelines and school practices on the one hand, and attempts by staff to meet the social and therapeutic needs of pupils with severe and complex disabilities on the other.

How do staff typically respond to challenging behaviours?

Teachers were asked to comment on who they thought was responsible for dealing with the pupil when he or she was behaving in the way described. Eight of the teachers in Phase I and six of those in Phase II thought they, alone, were responsible. Two teachers in Phase I and four in Phase II thought they shared responsibility with the head teacher. Some teachers seemed unsure and qualified their answers with comments such as, 'It depends' or 'It's a joint responsibility'.

As a precursor to questions about management strategies, teachers were also asked whether there was any pattern to the pupil's problem behaviour and whether they were able to predict likely occurrences. For both groups of teachers (Phase I and Phase II) about half thought that they could predict when the behaviour(s) were likely to occur. The most reliable indicators were 'situations' and 'times of day'.

Table 5.8

Is there any pattern to the pupil's challenging behaviour?

Behaviours are more likely to occur:	Phase I n = 11	Phase II N = 11
In certain situations	5	8
At certain times	6	3
In certain places	1	3
With certain people	2	2
Other	2	4

All four items were included as response options in the questionnaire.

Teachers who were interviewed gave the following examples of situations linked to changes in behaviours: 'He's calmer in a quiet environment'; 'He responds to changes in routine (with challenging behaviour)'; 'It's a response to a freer class-room routine'. Two teachers indicated lunch times were likely to be difficult. (This is presented under 'times' although the situation may also have been influential). Three teachers felt that a pupil's behaviour was likely to be better in the afternoons while one thought it was likely to be worse.

Teacher responses were explored by asking 'What do you do when the pupil behaves in the way you have described?' In the interview, respondents were asked about previous interventions and their efficacy. In the questionnaire, a list of possible responses was provided and they were simply asked to indicate which, if any, of their responses to challenging behaviour were considered effective. A similar question was asked in respect of responses from other staff.

Table 5.9
Teacher responses to challenging behaviour
Figures in parentheses indicate those who thought they response was effective

Type of response	Phase I n = 11	Phase II n = 11
Ignore/avoid the problem*	6(1)	8(4)
Divert/distract the pupil*	4(1)	8(4)
Remove the pupil from the situation*	3(2)	6(2)
Remove other pupils*	2(1)	0
Get help	0	4(1)
Verbal reprimands	5	1
Holding pupil/physical restraints	3	1
Physical prompts/guidance	3(1)	0
Reinforcement for 'good' behaviour	3(1)	1
Try to include pupil	1	0
Giving him a task	1	0
One to one working	2	0
Placing the pupil close to the teacher	0	1
Peer pressure	0	0

* Indicates items included as response options in the questionnaire.

Apart from the use of reinforcement, all of these responses represent reactions to difficult behaviour once it has occurred. For the teachers in Phase II, it is not clear how far this is a result of the way in which the questions were posed. However, it is significant that when the broader question about interventions was present during the interview, very few proactive strategies were described. It is also apparent that very few responses were considered effective. Of those respondents referring to a particular response, no more than 50% thought it made any difference. This has serious implications both for the pupils concerned and for teachers' feelings about their own competence and ability to produce a change.

Table 5:10 summarises the responses to challenging behaviours made by other members of staff.

Table 5.10
Responses of other staff to challenging behaviour
Figures in parenthesis show those responses thought to be effective

	Phase I N = 11	Phase II N = 11
Ignore/avoid the problem*	0	6(11)
Divert/distract the pupil*	1(1)	8
Remove the pupil*	1(1)	7(1)
Remove other pupils*	1(1)	0
Get help*	1	3
Team strategies	4	0
Trying to stop the pupil	2	0
Shouting	2	0

* Indicates items included as response options in the questionnaire.

Once again, the emphasis is upon reactive strategies, and very few respondents thought that their colleagues were being effective.

Teachers' feelings
We felt that it was important to explore teachers' feelings towards pupils who presented problem behaviour. In the interview we asked 'What are your feelings towards N when he/she has been behaving like this?' and then 'How do you deal with these feelings. Is there anyone in the school to whom you are able to talk?' In

the questionnaire we asked 'How do you feel when N is behaving like this?' and 'How do you deal with these feelings?' The feelings experienced by teachers as a consequence of working with pupils who present a challenge are described in Table 5:11.

Table 5.11

Teachers' feelings towards pupils who present challenging behaviour

	Phase I N = 11	Phase II N = 11
Angry*	4	1
Upset*	3	0
Stressed*	1	3
Anxious*	0	2
Afraid*	0	0
Frustrated*	7	8
Determined*	0	5
Inadequate	1	0
Helpless	1	0

* Indicates items included as response options in the questionnaire.

From the data, it is clear that teachers do experience strong emotions as a result of their work with pupils who present challenging behaviour. The most frequently cited feelings seem not to arise from the immediate impact of the behaviours, but rather the teachers' feelings of inadequacy and impotence to effect change. The number of Phase II teachers endorsing 'frustrating' and 'determined' is interesting insofar as it suggests that challenging behaviours can sometimes become a focus for a confrontation in which adults may perceive themselves as having a significant personal stake. This has important implications for in-service work designed to establish positive and appropriate attitudes among staff working with this group of pupils. Other comments included: 'He's a bloody nuisance at times'; 'fascinated'; and 'I think she's brilliant'.

The different ways in which teachers dealt with their feelings towards pupils who challenged, are summarised in table 5:12.

Table 5.12
Dealing with feelings aroused by challenging behaviour

	Phase I N = 11	Phase II N = 11
Talk to other members of staff	10	10
Become bad tempered	0	2
Bottle it up till later	2	0
Try not to think about it	1	1

All four items were included as response options in the questionnaire.

While it is encouraging to know that nearly all staff consulted, felt that they could talk to their colleagues about their feelings, there is concern about the absence of more formal systems to support staff (see sections on whole school approaches below). If not properly addressed, negative feelings are likely to have a number of adverse effects on staff performance and, either directly or indirectly, on the pupils for whom they are responsible. During the interviews other suggestions for dealing with strong emotional vibrations were: 'distance myself'; 'moan to my boyfriend'; 'go to the gym or the pub'.

Co-ordination within the school
As a prelude to an intervention study designed to promote a 'whole-school' approach, it was important to determine the extent to which staff were already involved in co-ordinated responses to pupils with challenging behaviour. The semi-structured interview and the questionnaire contained a number of specific questions on reporting incidents of challenging behaviour, maintaining records of challenging behaviour, formal assessment of the pupil concerned, communication of strategies and provision of staff support. The main methods of co-ordinating a school-wide approach to pupils who challenge are shown in Table 5:13.

From these data, there is little evidence of record keeping, co-ordination of effort, or systematic attempts to understand and respond to pupils who present problem behaviours. While it is encouraging that all the teachers in Phase I schools and nearly 50% of those in Phase II reported that other staff were informed of strategies for working with these pupils, the methods employed were mostly oral, for example 'word of mouth' (3), 'staff meetings' (2). Only five teachers indicated that written information was circulated to colleagues. Similarly, of those that indicated the availability of staff support during the interviews, two said this was 'informal'.

The overall impression is of loosely structured, often informal, systems which are available to staff if they wish to make use of them. There is a notable absence

Table 5.13

School procedures for responding to challenging behaviour

| | YES | | NO | |
	Phase I	Phase II	Phase I	Phase II
Incidents reported to head teacher	3	4	4	7
Teacher keeps records of incidents	7	5	4	6
Records kept by staff	3	4	8	7
Records used to understand challenging behaviour	0	1	11	10
Formal assessment during last three months	2	0	8	11
Other staff informed of strategies	11	5	0	6
School support for staff dealing with challenging behaviour	5	5	6	6

Phase I, N = 11; Phase ll, N = 11

'No response' (missing data) accounts for items where YES and NO figures for Phase I do not sum to 11.

of formal school-wide procedures for identifying and assessing the behaviours which pose problems, planning and communicating strategies to relevant members of staff, and providing effective systems of staff support.

Help from outside the school
In the past, special schools, in particular, have been able to count on help from a variety of different professionals and statutory agencies. With the changing role of local education authorities and the introduction of Local Management of Special Schools (LMSS), this is already beginning to change and is unlikely to continue in the future. We asked teachers what other agencies were involved in working to overcome the behaviours described and who was responsible for liaising with other agencies (Table 5.14).

For this group of teachers, there was remarkably little support or professional advice available from sources outside the school. The majority of teachers (eleven in Phase I and three in Phase II) saw it as the head's responsibility to liaise with these other organisations. However, as many as five teachers in Phase II felt that this was their responsibility.

Keeping parents informed
Finally, we asked about the role of parents and how teachers kept in touch with

Table 5.14
Other agencies involved with pupils who present challenging behaviour

	Phase I	Phase II
Social services	1	2
Schools medical officer	1	1
Family doctor	0	1
Educational Psychologists	3	4
Occupational Therapist	0	0
Speech therapist	0	1

All six items were included as response options in the questionnaire.

Other professional support staff referred to were an LEA support group (1), visits to hospital (1), residential unit staff (1), and parents (1).

parents. In both Phase I and Phase II schools, eight teachers (sixteen overall) said that they kept parents informed about the behaviours which they had described as problematic. The home-school diary was the most frequently used method, being employed by fifteen teachers overall. Only three teachers (all in Phase II) sent letters home and only two made telephone calls to pupils' parents. Two teachers in Phase I and five in Phase II indicated that parents visited the school. No teachers made visits to the homes of pupils. Nine teachers stated that parents asked them for advice about managing the pupil's behaviour and the same number reported offering advice to parents.

It is clear that while many teachers maintain contact with parents, there is relatively little opportunity for face-to-face contact and discussion. Nearly half of the teachers were asked for advice and a similar number offered it, although without greater face-to-face contact than is described here, it is difficult to see how it could be successful. We did not ask about the extent to which teachers felt they were able to help parents, but bearing in mind the general lack of optimism regarding the methods employed in schools, it would be surprising if the teachers felt particularly confident in this role.

Summary
In this chapter we have started to describe the process of collaboration with staff in schools including the first whole school meeting and the method of selecting pupils for involvement in the study. Following a description and an analysis of the behaviours which were identified as challenging, the chapter summarises the

information on staff reactions to pupils who challenge, existing methods of responding to problem behaviours, and sources of help and advice from inside and outside the school. In the following chapter, we turn to the next stage in the process of collaboration: the development and implementation of strategies for responding to challenging behaviours.

Chapter 6

DEVELOPING STRATEGIES FOR INTERVENTION

The information from the interview and self-report questionnaire, together with the data derived from classroom observation, provided a basis for a discussion about the challenging behaviour presented by the pupil and possible courses of action. Present at these Review Meetings were the two project staff, the child's teacher, one or more classroom assistants and the head or deputy head teacher of the school. Decisions regarding parental involvement during the project and invitations for parents to attend the Review Meetings were left to the head teacher and teaching staff. In the event, no parents attended the Review Meetings.

The discussion at the Review Meetings was informal and free ranging. The project team was concerned to create a supportive and non-judgmental climate in order that staff could speak freely without fear of criticism. The meetings had a number of aims:

(1) To carry into practice the idea of collaborative working between the project team and the school staff.

(2) To explore the significance of problem behaviours for the pupil, his or her peers and staff.

(3) To build on good practice where effective approaches to pupils' challenging behaviours had already been established.

(4) To make specific recommendations for further action where appropriate.

(5) To identify changes in classroom or school organisation required to support implementation of the recommendations.

To achieve these aims, the discussion was structured around six questions. Sheets of paper with the questions typed as headings and space for notes were distributed to all present at the meetings. After a brief summary of the main challenges presented by the pupil, the group worked through the following questions:

1. How do you think the situation appears to N?
This was deliberately introduced at the beginning of the meeting to encourage exploration of the causes and consequences of the behaviour from the *pupil's*

perspective. Teachers and classroom support workers found it quite difficult to move away from thinking about how the behaviour impacted on their own personal and professional needs and aspirations. In some cases, it was clear that this was the first time staff had been asked to look at a pupil's behaviour in this way. For the majority of pupils school staff described the pupils as experiencing confusion or having problems in making sense of what was happening around them.

The following are typical examples of comments from staff:

- 'Tony is disorganised and inconsistent. No cognitive strategies; not remembering'.

- 'Stephen often appears to be confused and to have difficulty in understanding social cues. Difficulty in communicating needs and wishes'.

- 'Nigel doesn't seem to realise the problems he causes although he seems to be very bright in some ways. Still seems to be lots of muddle and confusion in the way he sees the situation, particularly with comprehension of language'.

- 'When Mary behaves badly, either something has happened that she doesn't understand, or something has made her unhappy. Sometimes, it seems that she really doesn't want to behave like that, but she can't help herself'.

- 'John is very manipulative - he tries to alter the situation to achieve his aims. He's learned a number of ways of doing this to give him control over the situation. He is chaotic in his responses, but he doesn't seem upset or distressed'.

- 'Colin appears to be confused by all the people, noise and visual stimuli in the classroom'.

- 'Charles presents a constantly changing picture. Often appears to be confused, although it's difficult sometimes to identify any cause for his confusion'.

- 'It's difficult to tell how things appear to him. Ben is not getting as much attention as he wants. In classroom he doesn't cope well with changes in the environment'.

- 'Angela doesn't seem to make much sense of the situation. She seems to be confused by the noise and 'busyness' of the area. Her behaviour seems to be a response to all the confusion, although she seeks a predictable response from others'.

- 'Harry appears to be aware of the disruption he's causing and it sometimes seems to upset him, but he doesn't seem able to control it; no internal control'.

- 'Most of Carol's behaviours appear to be craving for attention, particularly screaming and aggression, although sometimes when she gets attention, she doesn't really seem to want it'.

2. What do you think N's needs are at this point?

This question was designed to link the preceding discussion of the pupil's perspective with subsequent proposals for interventions. This contrasts with more conventional thinking in schools which often leads to an assessment of pupil needs in respect of educational goals and objectives, for example, the need for independence or the ability to concentrate on materials selected by the teacher. This question always generated a great deal of discussion with contributions from both school and project staff. The notes from the meetings indicate a consensus arising from discussion. Typical statements were:

- Needs a structured day. Needs consistency of approach from staff.

- Needs clear expectations and structure. Needs stable relationships and trust. Needs tasks which build on his strengths.

- Needs to be left to sort things out; to be given space; help to express her emotions; activities which are relevant to her ability; a lot of structure.

- Needs a routine: predictable outcomes; structure; ways of making needs known; consistent approach.

3. How are present strategies helping?

This question initiated a positive discussion of existing strategies and ensured that new suggestions were incorporated as additions or extensions to what staff were already doing rather than something completely new.

4. What problems are associated with present strategies?

It was important to address the limitations of existing strategies before moving on to consider additional ways of working, both to avoid repetition of ineffective approaches and to understand the practical constraints imposed by classroom and school organisation. The responses to this question, mainly provided by school staff, are described in Table 6:1.

Problems associated with existing strategies

In the case of only one pupil did staff consider there to be no problems associated with current ways of responding to the challenging behaviour. For all other pupils, a number of difficulties were described. The most frequently expressed concerns

Table 6.1
Problems associated with existing strategies

	Number of Pupils (N=24)
Disruption to classroom activities	10
Demands on staff time	11
Injury/risk of injury to staff/pupils	8
Inhibits staff ability to meet needs of other pupils	6
Negative impact on pupil (restraint/upset/seclusion)	6
Staff experience frustration/stress	2
Consistent approach from staff	4
Strategies are ineffective	6
No problems	1

were about the disruption of other classroom activities, including efforts to teach other pupils and the demands which the intervention strategies placed upon staff time. A closely related issue was the teachers' ability to meet the needs of other pupils while, at the same time, trying to respond to pupils presenting a challenge. One third of teachers felt that they, or their pupils, were at risk of physical injury from the pupils who displayed challenging behaviour and a quarter thought that there were adverse consequences, such as isolation for the pupils on whom the interventions were focused. For one in every four pupils, teachers felt the interventions were ineffective.

The overall impression is of strategies which created numerous organisational and management problems and raised concerns about the well-being and education of all pupils including those receiving the interventions.

5. How do you think N's needs can be met?
This was the main focus for ideas about new ways of working with the pupil. Responses to this question formed the basis of all the project interventions. These are summarised in Table 6:2 and considered in more detail below.

6. What structures need to be in place in school for N's needs to be met?
This question was designed to help the group explore organisational changes which would be needed to support implementation and was particularly pertinent to the continuing role of the head teacher and other senior staff. Some of the responses were concerned specifically with aspects of classroom organisation, for example, establishing periods of one-to-one work. Others involved other staff, for example, when it was felt important that everyone should be able to employ a specific reactive management strategy thus ensuring consistency throughout the school. The relationship

between organisational characteristics of the school and the successful implementation of intervention strategies is discussed later in this chapter.

Table 6.2   Interventions: recommended and implemented

Each recommendation made at the Review Meetings is listed. Those which were subsequently implemented are shown in bold. The proportion of recommendations implemented for each pupil is indicated.

Phase I Schools

Charles

1. **Inform staff of the need to communicate clear expectations and establish predictable outcomes to reduce confusion.**

2. **Explain order of daily events using a story board.**

3. **Strategy to 'opt out' to be provided with a 'pass' and safe place to 'cool off'.**

4. To be offered a range of activities and possibly a special morning/ lunch time job.

5. **Prepare a written protocol for responding to 'crisis situations'.**

4/5

Mary

1. A structured day with transitions to new activities clearly marked.

2. Programme of activities appropriate to age and ability.

3. **Help to monitor her own behaviour - a 'pass' to use to avoid difficult situations (opting out).**

4. Structured language programme to develop expressive language skills.

1/4

Cliff

1. **Identification of preferred activities and best ways of interacting.**

2. Structured activities for a short period each day.

3. Reward system to include self-monitoring.

4. **Inform staff about preferred learning styles/styles of interaction.**

2/4

Carol

1. Structured programme of activities for short sessions each day.

2. Structured day with clear boundaries between different activities.

3. Improved communication skills through structured teaching.

4. Strategy for 'opting out' using a special chair.

5. Inform staff about new methods of working.

5/5

Colin

1. A structured programme of activities reflecting needs and interests.

2. A structured day emphasising a predictable sequence of events.

3. Opportunities for sensory exploration.

4. Developing communication skills in everyday settings.

5. A reward system for appropriate behaviour.

6. Support for staff working with Colin.

6/6

Harry

1. Building self esteem: error free learning, discussing relationships, being given responsibility.

2. A reward system for appropriate behaviour.

3. Inform other staff of the importance of simple direct instructions.

4. Develop appropriate ways of expressing needs using cards or pictures.

5. Programme to develop social skills; use another pupil as peer tutor.

6. Written programme for responding to 'crisis situations' to be prepared and circulated to other staff.

5/6

Stephen

1. **Introduction of a structured day**

2. **Establish a consistent approach from staff involving simple direct communication.**

3. **Develop interaction and relationship with one member of staff,**

4. **A programme for communication skills.**

4/4

Angela

1. A structured day with boundaries between activities clearly explained to Angela.

2. **Programme of activities which ensure success and are associated with rewards.**

3. **Regular one-to-one teaching sessions.**

4. **Opportunity to 'opt out' of activities involving large groups or lots of noise.**

3/4

Ben

1. **A programme of activities built around Ben's interests and strengths.**

2. **Joining other classes for some activities.**

3. Staff to clarify the distinction between 'care' and encouraging participation in educational activities.

4. Further exploration of reasons for screaming behaviour.

2/4

Robert

Admitted to psychiatric hospital; no further work possible.

Alan

1. A programme of activities which are within Alan's ability; the provision of tangible and social rewards.

2. Create opportunities for building interaction with a small number of adults, for example, at drinks time.

3. Establish predictable routines and expectations throughout the day.

4. Communicate information about methods of working with all staff.

5. Remove Alan's protective helmet when he does not head-slap.

6. Opportunities to leave classroom when in a frenzy: opting out.

5/6

Tony

1. Programme of activities which reflect interests and abilities; may need further exploration in view of Tony's very immature development.

2. Space and time for unstructured exploratory play, using soft play area.

3. Explore use of high sided chair to support Tony and encourage concentration on specific activities.

3/3

Nigel

1. Continue existing communication programme.

2. Develop communication programme to provide opportunities for choice and control.

3. Establish regular one-to-one teaching sessions.

4. Provide opportunities for withdrawal (opting out) from confusing situations.

5. Communicate sequence of events in the school day.

6. Inform staff of importance of structure and establishing clear expectations.

6/6

John

1. Change teaching groups so that he is with age peers.

2. Introduce a clearly structured day.

3. Improve organisation so that 'waiting times' at the beginning and end of lessons are minimised.

4. Programme to encourage social interaction.

5. Review activities which may be used to reinforce appropriate behaviour.

6. Communicate to other staff the importance of establishing clear expectations when working with John.

7. Change the way adults interact with John to avoid escalation of challenging behaviour.

6/7

Heather

Absent owing to illness throughout the period of intervention

Overall, 82% of interventions were implemented in Phase I schools.

Phase II Schools

Simon

1. Programme of structured activities which reflect Simon's interests and abilities, linked to clear rewards.

2. Reward system for appropriate behaviours linked to everyday activities.

3. Review of classroom seating arrangements to help overcome Simon's visual and auditory disabilities.

4. Explore the use of additional teaching aides for VI and HI.

5. Inform other staff about methods of working with Simon.

5/5

Michael

1. Social skills training.

2. Provide opportunities for practising social interaction.

3. Self-monitoring of inappropriate behaviour.

4. Introduce a system of rewards for appropriate behaviour.

5. Protocol for staff management of difficult behaviour and inform other staff of methods of working with Michael.

5/5

Martin

1. Structured programme to encourage development of communication skills.

2. Programme of activities designed to provide Martin with experience of success, and immediate rewards.

3. Clear rewards for appropriate behaviour.

4. Activities which provide Martin with short periods of independent play i.e. distant, rather than close, supervision.

5. Establish protocol for responding to aggression: inform all staff of agreed procedures.

6. Further assessment of language comprehension skills.

4/6

Jack

1. Inform staff of the importance of establishing clear expectations and providing immediate rewards for appropriate behaviour.

2. Programme of activities building on strengths and providing clear rewards.

3. Establish a structured and predictable sequence of daily events to ensure Jack is informed about any changes to the routine.

4. Investigate possible hearing and visual disabilities.

4/4

Mick

1. Clear system of rewards for appropriate behaviour, especially compliance.

2. Programme of activities based on interests and strengths.

3. Inform all staff of the importance of clear expectations and the provision of appropriate feedback for compliance.

4. Programme of activities for short session each day; to be provided by the same member of staff in one-to-one setting.

5. Establish written protocol for responding to non-compliance and aggression.

4/5

Neil

1. Programme of activities which reflect interests and strengths to be introduced for a short period each day.

2. Inform all staff of the importance of establishing clear expectations.

3. Establish a clear and direct system of rewards for appropriate behaviour.

4. Provide opportunities for choice during the school day.

5. Establish a clear sequence of daily events and activities which Neil can understand.

5/5

Ruth

1. Short activity sessions building on her strengths and interests; to be presented daily by same member of staff.

2. A system of rewards for appropriate behaviours.

3. Investigate links between behaviour and menstrual cycle; also medical reasons for frequent use of toilet.

3/3

Darren

1. Programme of activities building on strengths and interests.

2. Encourage communication; establish teaching programme.

3. System of rewards for appropriate behaviour: DRO for hand tapping.

4. Clean materials such as towels or flannels may provide a safer focus for mouthing, sucking and licking.

5. Inform all staff of new methods of working.

6. Investigate reasons for screaming.

7. Consider short periods of integration with pupils in mainstream school .

5/7

Adam

1. Programme of activities which reflect Adam's interests and strengths to be introduced for short daily sessions.

2. Opportunities for developing a relationship and interacting with one member of staff.

3. Written protocol for responding to aggression and stereotypic behaviours.

4. Opportunities for Adam to 'opt out'; provision of 'comfy corner'.

5. Provide activities for use during periods of 'opting out'.

6. Inform staff of the importance of clear and direct communication with Adam.

6/6

Clive

1. Programme of activities which will promote independence and choice.

2. System of rewards for appropriate behaviour: DRO for pinching.

3. Introduce activities to assist relaxation, for example, swimming and trampolining.

4. Teaching sessions to help Clive to adjust to his developing sexuality.

5. **Written protocol indicating strategies for responding to aggression.**

4/5

Chris

1. **Continue the existing strategy of ignoring inappropriate behaviour (e.g. throwing) and inform all staff.**

2. **Review existing teaching activities in the light of Chris's preference for manipulation/motor skills.**

3. **Encourage communication in ordinary activities.**

4. **Reward system (based on food rewards) for appropriate behaviour: DRO for pinching.**

5. Substitute alternative (hygienic) materials for surfaces usually licked.

6. Seek medical advice on possible causes of inappropriate behaviours.

3/6

Overall, 84% of recommendations were implemented in Phase II schools.

Interventions strategies proposed during the Review Meetings

Following the Review Meetings, the main recommendations were summarised and subsequently used as a basis for discussion with individual class teachers and support workers. Table 6:2 shows the recommendations made in respect of each pupil. The number of pupils involved in the project was reduced from 26 to 24 following the hospitalisation of one pupil and the absence through illness of another. The interventions which were subsequently implemented with support from the project team are shown in bold type. The proportion of interventions implemented is shown for each pupil and also for all pupils in Phase I schools and all pupils in Phase II schools. Overall, just over 80% of recommendations made at the Review Meetings were implemented excluding those for pupils who were withdrawn from the project.

All the recommendations arose from discussions during the Review Meetings. Inevitably, these were expressed in ways which reflected the concepts and language being used by teachers and care staff in the different schools and often described similar approaches using a variety of words and phrases. In order to expose the similarities and differences underlying these approaches, we have systematised and abbreviated the wording of many of the original recommendations.

Retrospectively, it is possible to see a number of common themes in strategies emerging from the one hundred and twenty or so specific recommendations. In Tables 6:3, 6:4 and 6:5 all the recommendations are summarised under three major headings: interventions which involve the whole school; those which are concerned with changes in the classroom; and, finally, proposed changes in adult/pupil styles of interaction. This is a *post hoc* approach to classification and it is quite possible that there are other equally valid ways of grouping the various recommendations. We have chosen this system of classification as we have found it particularly useful when talking about the project to teachers and classroom support workers.

School organisation and the whole school approach

In schools, the organisational structure is based upon the division of pupils into teaching groups or classes. Individual pupils are usually regarded as the responsibility of their class teacher who is also responsible for planning programmes of work and ensuring that each pupil receives a broad balanced curriculum which is directly relevant to his or her needs. Much of the daily work by pupils and teachers is carried out in the relative isolation of their own classrooms or teaching areas and there is seldom the need for formal communication between members of staff working with different groups about the performance of individual pupils. At most, this might happen at the beginning or at the end of a school year immediately before pupils are transferred from one teaching group to another. Most schools for pupils with severe learning difficulties do not have established procedures for exchanging information about the behaviour of individual pupils on a regular basis; when necessary, this is usually done informally in the staff-room over coffee or at lunch time.

The limitations of the 'classroom', as a coherent and relatively independent organisational unit, becomes apparent when dealing with pupils who present challenging behaviours. First and foremost, it may be difficult for teachers and their support staff to obtain appropriate help and advice. They may be reluctant to ask for help if this appears to undermine their professional credibility and, without a formal system for exchanging information, colleagues and senior managers may not be aware of the seriousness of the problems presented by pupils with challenging behaviour. Unless help is requested, other staff may be unwilling to infringe upon the class teacher's recognised sphere of responsibility, as their action might be seen as questioning or deliberately undermining his or her authority. It is also possible that, so long as a pupil with challenging behaviour is being contained in one classroom, other members of staff prefer not to become involved in working with extremely difficult and demanding pupils.

The relative isolation of teaching groups in most special schools means that, very often, teachers and their support staff have to manage as well as they can.

Inevitably, the quality of intervention is varied; some staff evolve effective methods which limit the impact of challenging behaviours and enable pupils to participate in some educational activities. Others adopt inappropriate management strategies or apply potentially useful methods inconsistently. Where pupils continue to present high levels of severely challenging behaviour over a considerable period of time, there is little doubt that this has serious adverse consequences for all those concerned, including staff and other pupils in the group.

The case of Ben illustrates how inappropriate management strategies can evolve in the relative seclusion of the classroom. Ben frequently cries or screams for no apparent reason. He seems to dislike group work and responds by biting and scratching other pupils. He has cerebral palsy and the physiotherapist has provided a standing frame with a small table attached to help him to improve his hand-eye co-ordination. When other pupils are engaged in group work, Ben is strapped into his standing frame and positioned some distance away, so that he cannot disrupt the activity.

Without additional support, Ben's teacher is doing her best to prevent him from disrupting her work with the other pupils. While Ben's behaviour is contained in this way, the teacher seems to be coping and there is no apparent need for advice or guidance from other members of staff. However, during the Review Meeting it was agreed that Ben needed a programme of activities which were more closely tailored to his individual needs. He should only be placed in the standing frame for short periods of time and it should never be used simply to restrict his movements.

Much of the time which pupils spend outside the base classroom is devoted to non-educational routines including playtimes, lunch break and extra curricular activities. Staff are required to provide group supervision rather than responding to individual needs. Consequently, it is appropriate that different members of staff are involved at different times and on different days. While this system may appear to work well for most of the time, it is extremely vulnerable in the presence of pupils who present challenging behaviours. Sometimes, the challenging behaviour will be totally unexpected and staff responses are influenced by their own reactions which may include surprise, anxiety and fear. In other situations, each member of staff evolves a particular method of dealing with the behaviour according to the setting or activity which is currently in progress. For example, Michael is reluctant to pass through doorways and will often become quite aggressive if he is persuaded to go into the dining hall at lunch time. Rather than face Michael's aggressive outbursts, lunch time supervisors allow him to sit at a small table in the corridor outside the dining hall where he eats his lunch alone.

There was already some concern among staff about this practice of isolating Michael from his peers. Once it was raised by one of the project team during a preliminary visit to the school, an alternative strategy was quickly established. This involved providing Michael with his favourite foods if he sat at a table in the dining room. He was initially allowed to sit on his own some distance away from the other pupils. Over time his table was gradually moved closer to the others.

Ad hoc responses may overcome the immediate challenge, but increase the likelihood of similar inappropriate behaviours occurring in the future. It is also likely that pupils will experience quite different responses to the same challenging behaviours. In the short term, this may be simply confusing, but over time, it is likely that the behaviour may come to serve different functions in different settings. For example, self injury or aggression towards others may represent attention seeking with some staff and yet enable the pupil to avoid specific tasks when interacting with other staff. The long term effect will be an increase in the range of events and adult behaviours which are associated with the occurrence of a particular challenge. Finally, as we have seen in the case of Michael, inappropriate ways of managing challenging behaviour may become accepted because they alleviate the problem in the short term, even though they are incompatible with the long term welfare of the pupil.

Whole school interventions
During the Review Meetings, a number of similar interventions involving a Whole School Approach were suggested (see Table 6:2). The most frequent strategies are described here (Table 6:3) with illustrative examples.

Table 6.3 Interventions which involve the whole school (Total = 34)

Inform staff of need to communication clear expectations:
Charles; Harry; Stephen; Nigel; John; Jack; Mick; Neil; Adam.   9

Provide written protocol for crisis management:
Charles; Harry; Michael; Martin; Mick; Adam; Clive.   7

Inform staff about new methods of working:
Cliff; Carol; Alan; Simon; Michael; Darren; Chris.   7

Request further assessment:
Ben; Martin; Jack; Ruth; Chris; Darren.   6

Placement with other groups of pupils:
Ben; John; Darren.   3

Provide support for staff: 2
Colin; Ben .

Informing staff of the need for clear expectations

Harry often engaged in attention seeking behaviour, sometimes refusing to co-operate with anything the staff were trying to do. Harry's teacher and classroom assistant recognised the need for consistency and took a very firm approach which was reasonably successful. However, other staff seemed unsure of the best way of responding and combined cajoling, reprimands, threats, promises and attempts to ignore Harry. The outcome was that Harry's behaviour deteriorated at lunch times and when he was being taught by other staff. When this was discussed at the Review Meeting, it was agreed that Harry's teachers and the classroom support worker would brief other teachers and, if necessary, give practical demonstrations of how to respond to non-compliance.

Individual circumstances could make sharing information with other members of staff particularly important. Neil was described as a child who, 'knows when he can play up most and get away with it'. Unfortunately, he was being taught by two different teachers employed on a 'job share'; one working during the morning and the other during the afternoon. The two teachers rarely met to discuss Neil's behaviour and, consequently, there was no established method of responding to the challenge he presented. The full time classroom support worker was aware of the lack of consistency, but felt that her status made it impossible to initiate a co-ordinated approach by the two teachers. The need for closer co-ordination was identified at the Review Meeting and the teachers agreed to give the classroom support worker greater responsibility in working with this particular pupil. Eventually, one of the teachers left the school and the other was appointed to a full-time position.

Written protocol for crisis management

Carol seems to use screaming and physical aggression as a way of getting attention. Her class teacher thinks that she responds positively if her outbursts are ignored. Unfortunately, other staff find this very difficult. When incidents involving other staff escalate, the class teacher has to intervene, which undermines her attempts to indicate to Carol that aggression is not an appropriate way to obtain attention. When this was raised at the Review Meeting, it was agreed that all staff would be provided with written instructions explaining exactly what they should do should Carol became physically aggressive.

Informing staff of new methods of working

Darren seems to want to explore everything with his mouth. He will try and eat or drink anything that he is able to reach and staff are concerned about the restrictions this places on the activities which Darren can take part in. They are also concerned that he might swallow something which is poisonous. During the Review Meeting it was suggested that Darren could be given specially selected items to suck and chew. If staff were able to control what Darren put in his mouth, there would be less chance that he would become ill and fewer restrictions would need to be placed on his participation in different activities. It was agreed that all staff would need to be informed of this strategy so that Darren would receive consistent encouragement for mouthing the selected items.

Placement with other groups of pupils

The challenges presented by John are so severe that he is placed in a class with only one other pupil (who also presents challenging behaviours) and a full time teacher and classroom assistant. John rarely sits down, is frequently aggressive and only concentrates for a few seconds at a time. His teacher has been reduced to adopting a strategy which can be summarised as 'coping and containment'. The stress and frustration of working with John for over a year have affected her health and she has only recently returned from a period of sick leave. The policy of isolating John in a small class with a very high teacher/pupil ratio was discussed at the Review Meeting. While the practical benefits for other staff and pupils was clear, it was felt that this approach might not be in the best long term interests of John, his class teacher or the school as a whole.

As part of the strategy for responding to the challenges presented by John, it was agreed that he needed a more varied range of activities in the company of his age peers. It was also agreed that all staff should take some responsibility for working with him and that a personal timetable should be designed indicating different activities for John throughout every school day and involving supervision from a number of different members of staff. All staff were briefed on the importance of keeping John fully occupied and communicating clearly what they wanted him to do.

Challenging behaviour and classroom organisation

While age or ability is a suitable criterion for dividing pupils in ordinary schools into classes, the arrangement of teaching groups in special schools is complicated by the very wide range of pupil-ability levels and the discrepancy between chronological age and developmental progress. Furthermore, many pupils experience additional disabilities including challenging behaviour. These factors almost inevitably lead to groups of pupils with widely different social and educational needs.

While most classes in SLD schools have relatively high staff-pupil ratios, work with individual pupils is only possible to the extent that other pupils in the class can be engaged in group activities. In situations where two or more pupils require individual attention, it is often extremely difficult for teachers and support workers to organise activities in order that all pupils are fully occupied. Pupils who resist involvement in group activities may, therefore, be left to their own devices during those periods when it is not possible to commit staff to working with them on a one-to-one basis.

The activities and lessons which make up a school day may seem to follow a structured and highly predictable sequence, at least from an adult perspective. Things may appear quite different to pupils with severe learning disabilities. They are likely to have considerable difficulty in distinguishing predictable temporal patterns within the ebb and flow of people, actions, noise, language and materials which meld together to make the school day. Unexpected changes in routine, long delays between activities or brief interruptions are all potential sources of confusion and frustration.

For many of the teachers in this study, the management of challenging behaviour appeared to be closely associated with issues of power and competence. Pupils who displayed inappropriate or disruptive behaviour were seen as undermining the teachers' authority in one of the most important areas of professional competence: classroom control. In responding to relatively minor challenges, teachers were reluctant to let pupils 'get the upper hand' or 'come out on top'. When responding to minor incidents, often occasioned by a pupil's difficulty with an educational or social activity, teachers frequently insisted that the task was completed and that the pupil had to wait for the teacher to terminate the activity. As a result, relatively minor 'protests' sometimes escalated into confrontations in which the challenge presented by pupils became more overt, and less easily managed. While teachers clearly did not feel that they should encourage inappropriate behaviours by 'giving in' when pupils began to protest, they often ended up having to deal with events which disrupted the whole classroom. At the same time, pupils were learning that low level 'challenges' were of little avail in escaping from difficult or frustrating situations while more extreme forms of 'challenge' were more likely to succeed.

An alternative strategy involves recognising the pupil's initial 'challenge' as a signal that he or she is not comfortable in that particular setting. Rather than insisting that a task is completed, an appropriate adult response might be to offer a choice between continuing with the activity or taking a short break. This makes it possible to resolve the situation while the challenge is at a relatively low level and provides the pupil with an opportunity to exercise some degree of personal control.

Classroom interventions

During the Review Meetings, a number of recommendations were made regarding classroom organisation (see Table 6:4). The most frequently occurring strategies are described here with illustrative examples.

Establishing a clear sequence of daily events

Charles often becomes agitated at the beginning or the end of an activity. This is particularly noticeable if there is a prolonged period of collecting materials and tidying up after a practical lesson such as art or technology. This is the time when Charles is most likely to grab a member of staff and engage in a cycle of increasing aggression. On one occasion, the male head teacher was summoned because the female class teacher felt unable to withstand the increasing levels of aggression displayed by Charles. Both the head and the deputy attempted to calm Charles and provide a sense of security by placing their arms around him and holding his hands firmly. This approach was only moderately successful. Charles' behaviour was contained and other members of staff and pupils were protected. On the other hand, the combined efforts of the head and deputy head to restrain Charles lasted for nearly one and a half hours and for much of this time they were struggling and wrestling with Charles on the floor.

Table 6.4   Interventions which involved the classroom

A. Changes in classroom organisation (Total = 21)

Establish clear sequence of daily events:
Charles; Mary; Carol; Colin; Stephen; Angela; Alan; Nigel; John;
Jack; Neil.   11

Provide opportunities to 'opt out':
Charles; Mary; Carol; Angela; Alan; Nigel; Adam (plus activities for
Adam during opt-out*)   7

Miscellaneous: John (reduce waiting times); Simon (review seating);
Simon (teaching aides).   3

B. Changes in curriculum (Total = 33)

**Introduce planned activities to address pupils' strengths
and needs:**
Charles; Mary; Cliff; Carol; Colin; Angela; Ben; Alan; Tony; Simon;
Martin; Jack; Mick; Neil; Ruth; Darren; Aileen; Clare   18

Structured teaching for language and communication:
Mary; Carol; Stephen; Nigel; Martin; Darren.   6

Communication/interaction in everyday settings:
Colin; Harry; Alan; Nigel; Michael; Chris.   6

Sensory exploration/exploratory play:
Colin; Tony; Martin.   3

At the Review Meeting it was agreed that it would help Charles if he had some way of knowing the sequence of events during each school day and what activity or lesson was taking place next. In view of Charles' interest in pictures, the staff decided to make a pictorial timetable which they could use to explain what was happening each day. Unfortunately, while this approach was being introduced, Charles' behaviour deteriorated at home and, during one particularly violent episode, he was admitted to hospital.

Providing opportunities to 'opt out'

Mary's temper tantrums seem to occur when something has happened which she doesn't understand or if she is upset. Her teacher commented, 'She doesn't really want to behave like that, but she can't help herself'.

It was agreed at the Review Meeting that it would help Mary if she had some way of expressing her confusion and distress before she had a full blown temper tantrum. The staff would then provide her with the opportunity to take a break and spend a few minutes sitting quietly by herself. Mary was taught to use a red card as a 'pass'. She carried the card with her and if the staff thought she was becoming upset they asked for the pass and then encouraged Mary to sit on a large cushion in a 'quiet corner'. Within a few days, Mary was able to use the card in response to a verbal cue, 'Do you want to take a break?' Initial fears that Mary would use the pass to 'opt out' of all activities proved groundless.

The curriculum and challenging behaviour

Pupils are placed in classrooms to facilitate teaching and the main role of the teacher is to enable all pupils to engage with the curriculum. This can pose special problems for pupils who present challenging behaviours. First, the pupil's challenging behaviour itself may make it difficult to determine his or her intellectual abilities and hence the appropriate level at which to present lesson activities. Secondly, many pupils with challenging behaviours appear to have little or no interest in activities which are planned and presented by adults. Thirdly, participation in group activities may be particularly problematic for the reasons already stated. For all these reasons, the presentation of the National Curriculum to pupils with challenging behaviours requires careful planning and a long term strategy.

It may be necessary to spend a considerable period of time observing the pupil to determine not only levels of ability but also the activities which he or she likes and dislikes. The curriculum may then be planned in order that it is introduced via the pupil's preferred activities and using tasks which are well within his or her range of abilities.

Organising and teaching pupils depends upon effective communication. Many pupils who present challenging behaviours have very poorly developed social skills and limited understanding of spoken language or alternative communication systems, for example, Makaton signs or Bliss symbols. For some pupils, it is tempting to see a causal link between poor communication and challenging behaviour.

Perhaps disorganised and disruptive behaviour is a response to the frustration and confusion which occurs when pupils are unable to express their own wishes or fail to make sense of the information and requests expressed by others. For pupils where this interpretation applies, formal teaching of social skills, spoken language or an alternative communication system should lead to more effective interactions with adults and concomitant reductions in inappropriate behaviours.

For pupils who do not respond well to structured teaching, it may be necessary to create opportunities for learning about communication in more naturalistic settings, for example, at the beginning or end of activities or during social routines such as the mid-morning break for refreshments. Creating opportunities to practice communication outside formal teaching activities also ensures that new skills are used in situations which matter to the pupil. For example, a child who has learned the names of food items needs to be placed in a position to learn that the name can be used as a request and that this is a socially acceptable way of getting what you want. Needless to say, this understanding of the way in which language is used depends upon adults being prepared to respond to pupil requests. This may require a considerable effort when previous interactions have been built around adult attempts to control and contain pupil behaviours. During the review meetings recommendations were made regarding the curriculum for pupils who presented a challenge. Illustrative examples are described below.

Planned activities to address pupils' strengths and needs
Ruth's behaviour is so chaotic that it has a major impact on everything else that happens in the classroom. She spends much of the time moving around and twirling and will often bite and pinch for no apparent reason. Staff find it difficult to know what activities will appeal to her. She masturbates more intensely and more frequently than previously and it was suggested that this may be due to boredom or a response to some undetected source of stress. The impact of Ruth's behaviour is so great that there are many periods during the day when staff are unable to organise structured activities.

At the Review Meeting, it was agreed that a full daily programme of activities should be established for all the pupils in the class, and that these would be designed in the light of what was known about Ruth's interests and abilities in order that she could be fully involved. It was recognised that the classroom staff would need advice and practical help to develop and introduce a full range of activities.

Darren has frequent and inexplicable screaming tantrums. One of the biggest problems for staff is getting him to participate in classroom activities. Stereotypic hand-tapping and mouthing often seems to 'get in the way' when staff are trying to work with him. One of the recommendations at the Review Meeting was that staff should develop a selection of activities which matched Darren's interests and it was suggested that activities which involved manipulation might help to reduce his repetitive hand movements.

Structured teaching about language and communication
Martin shows aggression by pulling at the hair and clothes of people. Staff are unsure whether this is motivated by attention seeking or reflects excitement and confusion. However, if he is warned verbally, Martin will often refrain from grabbing and pulling. He works well in formal teaching settings and has learned some Makaton signs which he uses to make his needs known. At the Review Meeting it was agreed that work needs to be carried out both to assess his understanding of language and to teach expressive language skills. With better language skills, he would be in a better position to request attention from adults without having to grab them.

Communication/interaction in everyday settings
Michael engages in noisy bouts of verbal aggression particularly when staff make demands or if he is required to participate in group teaching sessions. Staff think that Michael uses swearing and abusive behaviour to try and avoid, or at least delay, participation in teaching activities. It also seems to occur when he is placed in unusual or slightly intimidating social situations.

At the Review Meeting, it was agreed that Michael needed to learn more appropriate ways of expressing his reluctance to engage in formal teaching activities. It was also felt that he needed an opportunity to practice and gain confidence in using social interaction skills in a variety of everyday settings.

Cliff clearly differentiates between the activities he will engage in and those which he actively resists. For example, he refuses to sort money or participate in any activities which involve writing or signing, although his teacher feels that he is probably capable of making progress in both of these areas. As a result, the teacher feels very frustrated by her inability to work effectively with Cliff. At the Review Meeting it was suggested that Cliff should be encouraged to express his choices using Makaton symbols, thereby emphasising the control he can achieve through conventional methods of communication.

Interventions concerned with teacher-pupil interactions
The quality of the relationship which exists between adults and pupils invariably has a profound impact upon teaching. It is also a crucial component of many intervention strategies designed to address challenging behaviour.

The challenges presented by many of the pupils in this study seemed to arise in situations where they were unsure of how to respond or were unwilling to participate in different kinds of social interaction. Informal social interactions are governed by a large number of 'unwritten rules' which enable people to communicate verbally and non-verbally. With only limited understanding of these 'rules', pupils with severe learning disabilities can easily become confused and overwhelmed when other people try to engage them in relatively simple interactions.

In contrast to the apparent lack of structure in many informal social interactions, teaching activities often impose a relatively rigid set of expectations and 'appropriate' behaviour may be defined within quite narrow boundaries. For example, the teacher is likely to determine both the task and the kind of response which will count as success. Some pupils with severe learning disabilities find such situations easier to cope with compared to casual social interactions, because the 'rules' are simpler and more clearly defined. Others find the imposition of a formal structure intimidating and a source of stress. Some pupils with very few social skills may even find it difficult to understand how they are supposed to respond in structured teaching sessions. Participation in group teaching activities is particularly problematic because it requires a combination of social skills; pupils must be able to engage in both the informal social interactions which constitute 'being a member of group' and respond to the more specific demands of an educational activity designed to elicit predetermined responses.

The provision of a system of rewards for appropriate behaviour is one way of simplifying social interactions. A reward marks appropriate behaviour in a way which is likely to be significant for the pupil. At the same time the Law of Effect (which states that behaviours which are reinforced will get 'stronger') increases the likelihood that the pupil will, in future, display similar behaviours in similar situations. The provision of rewards contingent upon specific behaviours may, therefore, help the pupil to play an appropriate part in simple social interactions even though he or she does not understand the social significance of the behaviour. To the extent that there is an increase in the frequency of behaviours which are both appropriate and predictable, teachers may also begin to feel more confident about engaging the pupil in social interaction.

Eventually, the pupil may begin to recognise the relationship between the behaviour which elicits the reward and other adult social behaviours. At this point, the pupil is in a position to explore his or her ability to exercise control over the interaction by 'trying out' different kinds of behaviour. This may include not responding with the target behaviour, to see what happens; trying a completely different behaviour which may be regarded as 'challenging' by staff; or copying other social behaviours displayed by staff or pupils. Clearly, the way in which staff respond to this kind of 'social exploration' will have crucial influence on the pupil's growing understanding of the way in which different behaviours can contribute to social interaction and his or her willingness to explore and experiment.

Reward systems may be helpful in clarifying the teacher's expectations and encouraging pupils to respond appropriately to both informal social interactions and to more highly structured teaching settings, especially when this involves regular one-to-one sessions with the same member of staff.

Interventions based upon teacher-pupil interactions

During the Review Meetings, a number of recommendations were put forward which involved developing the interactions between adults and pupil. The most frequently occurring strategies are illustrated here with examples from the pupils involved in this project.

Table 6.5
Interventions which involve changes in teacher/pupil interactions
(Total = 26)

Social skills and relationships:

Angela; Nigel; Adam; Mick; Harry; Stephen; Alan; John; Michael;
Neil; (Harry: other strategies to build confidence and self esteem*)   10

Introduce system of rewards:

Cliff; Colin; Harry; John; Simon; Michael; Martin; Mick; Neil; Ruth;
Darren; Clive; Chris.   13

Identify improved interactional styles:

Cliff; Chris; John.   3

Other pupil focused interventions (Total = 7)

Remove helmet	-	Alan
Special chair	-	Tony
Monitoring own behaviour	-	Michael
Substitute materials for mouth/licking		Darren; Chris
Relaxation	-	Clive
Sexuality awareness	-	Clive

NB *Where more than one recommendation per pupil is made in a single category, this has only been counted once to compile the total number of interventions.

Developing social skills and relationships

Angela seems to have difficult in making sense of much of what goes on around her. She seems confused by activity changes during the school day and also by the demands made upon her by adults in structured teaching sessions.

The Review Meeting recommendations included helping Angela to understand the sequence of activities during the school day. It was also felt that she would benefit from regular opportunities to engage in one-to-one teaching with one member of staff. These sessions would provide a clear teaching structure with a high density of rewards for appropriate behaviour. The aim would be to help Angela understand what was expected of her in formal teaching situations.

Mick often seems quite keen to engage in teaching activities but, for no apparent reason, will sometimes become unco-operative; in these situations, pressure from staff often results in displays of aggression. Mick is very aware of other pupils and often gets upset if they use materials or implements he regards as 'his possessions'. The staff feel that Mick's behaviour often prevents him from learning and showing his true ability.

After discussion at the Review Meeting, it was agreed that Mick needed regular periods of one-to-one teaching away from other pupils. It was felt that Mick needed to experience success in a highly structured teaching situation where expectations and consequences for compliance were clearly signalled.

For much of the time Stephen appears confused. He seems to have great difficulty in understanding social cues and, as a result, he often prefers to stay away from the usual classroom activities. On the other hand, he often seeks contact with adults and will participate in interactions which he has initiated. The Review Meeting recognised the need for Stephen to learn more about social interaction before he could participate in formal teaching sessions. It was, therefore, recommended that he was involved in regular one-to-one sessions with the same member of staff. There was to be no formal objective for these sessions other than to help Stephen to learn more about social interaction.

Improved adult/pupil styles of interaction

Staff regard John as manipulative. They feel that his challenging behaviour has developed in ways which enable him to control situations, particularly when he is asked to do something he doesn't like. John often gets his own way by being aggressive; if he is not allowed to have his own way, his behaviour increases in intensity. Staff are aware that they are contributing to John's problems by allowing him to use aggression as a way of avoiding activities. When these concerns were discussed at the Review Meeting, it was agreed that the classroom staff needed to change completely the way in which they interacted with John. Rather than let him use aggression to 'negotiate', it was decided that, in future, when he showed any aggressive behaviour, he would be moved quietly but firmly to a 'quiet area' outside the classroom. After a few minutes he would be allowed to return provided he did not display any further aggression. In view of John's tendency to run away, a member of staff would be with him at all times.

Chris seems to become angry when he is prevented from doing things. One of the triggers for pinching is an adult saying, 'No'. When this was discussed at the Review Meeting, it was agreed that all staff be asked to avoid direct confrontations with Chris including the use of the word 'No'. Staff were to explore other ways of interacting with Chris and less confrontational methods of steering him towards appropriate activities.

Introduce a system of rewards

Alan engages in regular high frequency self injury. It is not clear whether head banging occurs in response to situations he wishes to avoid, or as a means of gaining attention. The staff find Alan's head banging very distressing but are unsure how to respond. As a result, Alan is confronted with a variety of responses including reprimands, cuddles and physical restraint and being ignored.

In order to overcome inconsistent staff reactions to Alan's self injury, the Review Meeting recommended that all staff adopted a simple reward system. Head banging was to be ignored. Clear rewards were to be presented when he initiated social interaction and when he behaved appropriately (without head banging) in social situations, for example, at drinks time.

Simon lacks any interest in social interaction and prefers to be left alone to play with a box of Lego toys. He seems to avoid tasks deliberately which could result in success or failure, and staff find it extremely difficult to work out his true level of ability. One of the recommendations at the Review meeting was that Simon should be gradually introduced to a range of simple but highly structured tasks. Compliance was to be rewarded with opportunities to play with the box of Lego toys. Whereas previously the Lego toys were always available and 'kept Simon out of trouble', it was agreed that, in future, these would only be available as a reward for co-operation and compliance.

Summary

In this chapter, we have described the process by which specific challenges presented by each pupil were considered at the Review Meetings. Together, members of the school staff and the project team worked through a set of questions designed to encourage an examination of challenging behaviours from a pupil's perspective. The strengths and weaknesses of existing response strategies were considered before a detailed set of recommendations were agreed for each pupil. A relatively high proportion (over 80%) of these recommendations were subsequently implemented by teachers and classroom assistants with support from members of the project team.

Retrospectively, it was possible to classify the interventions into three categories:

- Those concerned with changes in school organisation

- Those concerned with classroom management and curriculum planning

- Those which focused on teacher/pupil interactions.

The chapter includes a discussion of some of the educational and organisational features of special schools which influence the way in which staff respond to challenging behaviours. A number of examples which illustrate the way in which specific interventions were implemented with individual pupils are provided. Finally, it is possible to identify those interventions which were recommended most frequently at the Review Meetings. While it is important to emphasise that each intervention was derived from a detailed examination of the possible cause of each challenging behaviour, it is, nevertheless, instructive to consider the top ten positive approaches.

Table 6:6   Top ten positive approaches

1. Help child to establish positive relations with one adult

2. Formalise appropriate and inappropriate behaviour using a system of rewards

3. Introduce planned activities, matched to pupil's strengths and interests

4. Focus on teaching language and communication

5. Encourage language and communication for meeting individual needs in everyday settings

6. Help the child to anticipate the sequence of daily events and activities

7. Provide opportunities for the child to 'opt out' of activities

8. Convey adult expectations clearly and provide consistent feedback

9. Ensure all staff are aware of new methods of working

10. Provide a written protocol which describes how to respond to each challenging behaviour.

* Each approach was recommended for at least 6/24 pupils.

One important conclusion to be drawn from this summary of the most frequently recommended interventions is that they are not technically sophisticated or particularly novel. In many respects, they reflect what many teachers regard as 'everyday good practice' when working with pupils with severe learning disabilities.

The second conclusion is that these strategies are more than 'applied common sense' or a distillation of practical classroom experience. They draw directly on the theories and the applied research described in Chapter 3. To this extent, they offer a template for translating clinical research into improved educational practice for those working with pupils who present challenging behaviours (Harris, 1995).

Chapter 7

CONSTRAINTS ON INTERVENTION STRATEGIES AND OUTCOMES FOR PUPILS

In this chapter, we begin by looking at some of the factors which affected the introduction of new methods of working with pupils selected for involvement in this study. In the second part of the chapter we consider the extent to which the intervention strategies were associated with changes in the occurrence of challenging behaviours. Following the structure established when describing the interventions, we consider the positive and negative influences on implementation with respect to the school, the classroom and individual teacher and pupil characteristics.

The school

School organisation and the extent to which this could respond flexibly to the requirements of specific intervention strategies was a major influence on the implementation of new methods of working with pupils who challenged. In some cases, school organisation contributed to the successful implementation of new approaches, while in others a lack of co-ordination, inflexibility or unforeseen circumstances hindered the introduction of new methods of working.

Examples of school organisation which had a positive impact on interventions

- In Bright School, the head and deputy arranged release time for classroom staff to meet with members of the project team.

- In Happy School, Angela was moved to a senior teaching group which provided a quieter and more structured environment.

- In Pleasant School, the involvement of Nigel in the project coincided with internal reorganisation and closure of the 'behavioural unit' which had, hitherto, been used for Nigel and one other pupil. Senior staff saw the project as an opportunity to promote change.

- In Joyful School, Michael was allowed to stay with a group receiving education in social and independence skills as part of the intervention strategy.

- In Lively School, cover was arranged so that Jack's former teacher could work alongside his present teacher to develop a varied programme of teaching activities.

- In Lively School, time was made available for Mick's classroom assistant to discuss progress with the project team at regular intervals.

- In Cheerful School, the head and deputy arranged for classroom staff to be released for additional training in behavioural recording.

Examples of school organisation which had a negative impact on interventions

- In Friendly School, Mary moved to a less structured FE unit which made the introduction of a structured programme of activities, including language teaching, more difficult.

- Staff changes in Cliff's classroom delayed the introduction of a structured programme of activities.

- In Happy School, Angela's move also meant that she was placed with two other pupils who presented severe challenging behaviour. The teacher appointed to this class was in her probationary year.

- In Merry School, a history of unhappy staff relations made it difficult to communicate intervention strategies and the head teacher was unable to arrange for release time for staff directly involved in the project to meet with the project,team. Appointment of a probationary teacher to work with long serving classroom assistants posed problems for introducing new methods of working.

- When Alan was moved to a new class during the project, the teacher was unwilling to carry on with the strategies which had been introduced.

- In Joyful School, the intervention strategies were frequently disrupted by school activities such as trips and concerts. Priorities were not clearly established.

- In Jolly School, two new pupils, both presenting severe challenging behaviour, joined Adam's teaching group during the project.

- Staff working with Ruth experienced difficulties in arranging time for liaison with the project team, although this improved with the appointment of a new deputy head.

In reviewing the impact of school organisation on intervention strategies, it is clear that the commitment of senior staff played a crucial role. First, they were influential in creating a 'climate for change' by the overt support they expressed for the project and the extent to which they explicitly linked the success of the project with long term benefits for staff and pupils in the school. Secondly, they were able to act as catalysts for change by ensuring that key aspects of school organisation were modified to accommodate the proposed interventions. This included arranging for staff directly involved in implementing change to be released for meetings with the project team and co-ordinating pupil placements to facilitate new methods of working. In some schools a failure to consider the impact of whole-school activities, such as concerts and sports days, resulted in considerable disruption of carefully planned intervention strategies and additional confusion for the pupils concerned. As Fullan comments, 'change is produced ... not merely by having change facilitators in school, but by how well the change facilitators and principals (head teachers) work together as a change facilitation team' (1991, p.156).

The classroom

For most of the pupils concerned, the classroom was the most important context for introducing new methods of working. It is, therefore, not surprising that there were numerous classroom factors which affected how successfully the Review Meeting recommendations were implemented.

Examples of classroom organisation which had a positive impact

- The staff working with Carol were keen to work together to develop a consistent approach and to consider how this could be coordinated with their work with other pupils in the group.

- The staff working with Harry worked well together as a team and had already established a highly structured and consistent approach involving all the pupils in the group.

- Nigel's teacher had already introduced a communication skills programme which was subsequently integrated with other strategies proposed at the Review Meeting.

- In Jolly School, the staff in Darren's class and those in Adam's class were keen to work together as a team and to develop a consistent approach.

- During a period of sick leave by Mick's teacher, the classroom support worker was able to take over responsibility for implementing intervention strategies.

Examples of classroom organisation which had a negative impact

- The staff working with Cliff disagreed about the reason for his difficulty in responding to planned educational activities and the class teacher was not able to organise a team meeting to discuss this.

- In Colin's classroom, it became clear during the project that there were considerable unresolved management and personal issues which affected the working relationship between the class teacher and the support workers.

- Staff working with Ben and Alan and Tony disagreed about the reason for their challenging behaviours and the best way of responding .

- The project team disagreed with classroom staff about Martin's ability to understand language.

- In Lively School, two teachers, working half a day each, shared responsibility for implementing new approaches for working with Neil.

- Classroom assistants appointed to work exclusively with Chris and Ben made it difficult to involve other classroom staff in interventions and to integrate new methods of working with ongoing classroom activities.

The autonomy experienced by classroom teachers and their freedom to organise educational activities within the classroom proved to be both a benefit and a constraint on the introduction of new methods of working. Where there was already a strong partnership between teachers and their support workers and where a well planned and structured approach to teaching was already in place, the proposals from the Review Meeting were likely to be welcomed and enthusiastically applied. In classrooms where lines of responsibility between teachers and their support workers were poorly defined or fractured as a result of personal differences, communication was often difficult. In such settings, a co-ordinated team approach was rarely seen and this, in turn, resulted in poor planning and weak organisation. Against this background, the introduction of new methods of working with pupils who presented a challenge was problematic. As Fullan aptly comments, new ways of working are unlikely to succeed when we 'introduce changes without providing a means to identify and confront situational constraints and without attempting to understand the values, ideas and experiences of those who are essential for implementing any changes' (1991, p.97). This is nowhere more apparent than in the special school classroom.

Pupils and teachers
Ultimately, the success or failure of interventions is tied to the ability of individual members of staff to initiate different approaches. In this project we were specifically concerned with ways of working and interacting with individual pupils. The qualities and characteristics which staff brought to the task of implementation

sometimes had a particularly powerful influence on the outcome. Similarly, pupil characteristics over and above the challenging behaviours which identified them as candidates for involvement in the project, occasionally made a significant difference to the introduction of new approaches.

Teacher and pupil characteristics which had a positive influence on interventions

- Carol's teachers arranged planning meetings in their own time out of school hours.

- Stephen's teacher, although in her probationary year, demonstrated enthusiasm, determination and considerable skill in working with three pupils with severe challenging behaviour.

- Michael moved to a new residential accommodation which provided a more adult and appropriate environment outside school.

Teacher and pupil characteristics which had a negative influence on interventions

- Charles and Robert were both admitted to hospital during the course of the project.

- Colin's teacher had been under considerable stress owing to his behaviour and this resulted in numerous short absences.

- Tony's teacher and Mick's teacher were absent owing to illness for several short periods during the project.

- Senior staff had already recognised that John's teacher was under considerable stress because of his severely challenging behaviour, and the project was viewed as a 'last chance' for the school to develop effective ways of responding to him.

- Simon was frequently absent through illness during the period of intervention.

- Jack's mother was taken into hospital and he was provided with respite care during the period of intervention.

- Ruth's teacher experienced considerable stress for personal and professional reasons during the project, which had a pronounced effect on his ability to introduce the proposed interventions.

- Adam's teacher was only recently appointed and had no previous experience of working with pupils with severe learning difficulties or of managing the work of two classroom support workers.

- Chris's teacher was appointed as a temporary 'supply teacher'. This was her first post after returning to teaching following a number of years in another career.

Clearly unforeseen absences by both staff and pupils had a significant impact on the implementation of the new methods of working. Other important teacher qualities were experience, the way in which they responded to the stress of working with pupils who challenge on a long term basis and less tangible qualities such as, enthusiasm and a belief in their own ability to bring about change.

This analysis draws attention to the overriding importance of ensuring that teachers are appropriately trained for working with pupils with severe disabilities. Working effectively with pupils who display challenging behaviour should, in future, be recognised as an essential aspect of professional competency, and strategies for responding to pupils who present severely challenging behaviour should be a major component of the in-service training available to all teachers in SLD schools. Fullan points out that school change is inextricably linked with staff development and training. For this reason, school change projects create an ideal opportunity for staff training and they provide concrete opportunities for learning new skills, and continuous staff support (at least for the duration of the project) and regular meetings with peers and others, around agreed topics and objectives.

Summary
The three 'levels' of school organisation (teacher/pupil, classroom and whole school) all play an important part in the introduction of change. The outcomes for each pupil involved in this project were determined by a unique combination of factors over and above the quality of the interventions which were recommended at the Review Meetings. It is impossible to determine the relative impact of each contributory factor or the extent to which the outcome might have been improved in slightly different circumstances. However, this descriptive analysis does suggest the conditions under which improved methods of working with pupils who challenge are most likely to flourish.

It is perhaps inevitable that, in seeking to understand the special needs of a small group of pupils, a project of this kind will establish a relatively narrow focus. However, it is also important to recognise the diverse needs of other pupils in these schools and the many other concerns and responsibilities which lay claim to teachers' time and energy during an ordinary school day. The interventions described represent the work which teachers and support workers were asked to take on, over and above their teaching commitments to other pupils.

It is often suggested that, by and large, teachers are driven by different motives and priorities compared to the 'agents of change' who initiate and facilitate intervention projects but who eventually go away leaving staff and pupils to 'carry on the good work'. Fullan suggests that 'One of the prevailing feelings that characterise the psychological state of teachers and teaching is 'uncertainty'- teachers are not sure whether they have made any difference at all' (1991, p.121). This uncertainty arises partly from a concern with individual pupils, partly from the unyielding pressure to attend to practical issues in the 'here and how' and partly from the myriad of environmental influences which together contaminate any single action by the teacher. It stands in stark contrast to the emphasis placed on objective evidence and the delineation of systematic relationships which typifies research.

Finally, it is worth considering the claim that researchers or 'change agents' pursue change in schools for rather different reasons and derive different benefits from positive outcome compared to teachers. Fullan suggests that there is an imbalance between the effort expended in establishing change and the benefits which accrue to teachers and researchers when change is successful. ' ... those who advocate and develop changes get more rewards than costs, and those who are expected to implement them (i.e. teachers) experience many more costs than rewards ... (This) ...goes a long way in explaining why the more things change the more they remain the same: if change works, the individual teacher gets little credit; if it doesn't the teacher gets most of the blame' (1991 p.127). In terms of the present study, this is a timely warning against simplistic interpretations about why some interventions were successfully implemented and others were not.

In the preceding discussion, we have tried to present a balanced account of the diverse factors which affected the introduction of new ways of working. Successful and unsuccessful implementations are influenced by a combination of multiple interacting variables located at three distinct 'levels' within the school. The more of these variables we are able to describe and control, the greater the chances of developing improved methods of working in the future. The challenge may appear to be located in a single pupil but the implementation of intervention strategies is always likely to be an issue which demands the involvement and commitment of the whole school. Furthermore, if Fullan is right about the mismatch between the costs and potential benefits arising from collaborative school-based research, future work must give greater attention to the relationship which exists between teachers and those who seek to improve teaching practice. Full collaboration between teachers and 'facilitators' will only be achieved when the costs and benefits of change are seen to be equally shared.

CHANGES IN PUPIL BEHAVIOUR

Recording behaviour in the classroom

Classroom based behaviour recording was employed for two reasons. First, behaviour recording, based on direct observation, is an integral part of any systematic approach to understanding and responding to pupils with difficult or inappropriate behaviours. Secondly, direct observation provides the best evidence that the work of school staff, with support from the project team, resulted in changes in specific problem behaviours. Reductions in clearly identified challenging behaviours provide one important measure of the success of the project. Other equally important outcome measures are discussed in the next chapter.

Different methods of direct observation were employed by the project team and by teachers:

Classroom observation by a member of the project team: one member of the project team spent time observing in all classrooms where there were pupils participating in the project. These observations took place prior to the review meeting and were repeated after implementation of the intervention strategies. The dates of the observation sessions by the project teams and classroom teachers in Phase I and Phase II schools is shown in Appendix 2.

The focus of the observations was the target child and, specifically, the behaviours which had been identified by the teacher as presenting a challenge. (These were recorded during a face-to-face interview for pupils in Phase I schools and by means of the self- report questionnaire for pupils in Phase II schools). It was also possible to make general observations about the behaviour of other pupils, staff approaches to classroom organisation, styles of interaction and the efficacy of existing methods of responding to problem behaviours. This enabled the project staff to make a positive contribution to the subsequent Review Meeting where intervention strategies were planned.

No attempt was made to interact with pupils or participate in classroom activities during the periods of observation. When pupils initiated interactions, the observer responded naturally but refrained from actions which would extend or intensify the exchange. A long-hand transcript of activities and the behaviour of the target pupil was prepared for each successive five minute time interval.

Teacher records: Since the project aimed to establish methods of working which could be maintained in schools with only minimum support from external agencies, it was considered essential that staff were involved in behaviour recording. All teachers responsible for target pupils were provided with record sheets and asked to keep a tally of the frequency or duration of up to three behaviours they had already identified as presenting a significant challenge. Examples of the record sheets are provided in Appendix 1. Teachers were asked to undertake recording of pupils' challenging behaviours before the initial Review Meeting and again after a period of implementing the proposed interventions. The time intervals between pre-intervention and post-intervention recording are shown in Appendix 2.

To overcome some of the practical difficulties arising from the additional demands of systematic recording, a flexible approach to time sampling was adopted. Teachers were asked to record for intervals of fifteen minutes. Five fifteen-minute intervals per day over five consecutive days was suggested as a schedule. In practice, teachers and classroom assistants adjusted recording sessions to fit in with daily routines and other activities. This arrangement provided project staff with little control over which activities and times of the day were selected for recording, and it is highly unlikely that the information provided was free from various forms of bias. We considered that this disadvantage was outweighed by the overriding concern to work in partnership with teachers and to establish procedures which could be accommodated as part of ordinary teaching practice.

Insufficient pre-and post-intervention recording was carried out by teachers in Phase I schools to justify analysis. Before teachers in Phase II schools were asked to carry out pre-intervention recording, additional training was provided for staff directly involved in the project, although in some schools, other members of staff also asked to attend. In Phase II schools, teacher recording was completed pre-and post-intervention for ten of the eleven pupils concerned. The dates of the first and last recording session pre-and post-intervention are shown in Appendix 2.

Results of classroom observation by the project team

The observation transcripts were scanned for the same behaviours which had been selected for observation and recording by classroom teachers. In most cases, these behaviours were derived from the information provided during interview (Phase I schools) or from the self-report questionnaire. For a small number of pupils, preparations for teacher recording indicated that a more specific target behaviour should be analysed or, in one or two cases, that behaviours previously not considered as a 'high priority' should be given greater attention.

Table 7:1 shows the total duration of pre-and post-observations for each pupil, expressed as the number of five minute intervals. Duration of observations varied from 45 to 410 minutes with a mean of 158 minutes pre-intervention and 100 minutes post-intervention. The table also shows absolute the frequency of target behaviours as well as frequency per five minute interval. This is referred to as 'rate of occurrence'. Where rate of occurrence is a figures less than 1, the average frequency is less than once every five minutes; where it is greater than 1 it indicates a frequency of more than one occurrence per five minute interval. Two behaviours, rapid self injurious slapping, and continuous periods of crying, shown by one pupil (Alan) are presented in terms of the number of five minute intervals during which there was any occurrence of this behaviour. The 'rate of occurrence' figures for these behaviours reflect the percentage of five minute intervals during which the behaviour was observed.

Table 7.1
Behaviour measurements derived from classroom observations by project staff

Only behaviours for which data is available pre and post are included i.e. zero frequency pre and post are not entered

School/ Pupil	Behaviour	F/D	Number of Intervals		Pre Freq. rate		Post Freq. rate		Change
			Pre	Post					
Joyful									
Michael	Noises	F	31	20	20	.64	0	0	decrease
	Non-compliance	F	31	20	7	.22	0	0	decrease
	Inappropriate - greetings	F	31	20	2	.06	0	0	decrease
Martin	Throwing	F	18	19	0	0	2	.10	increase
	Pulling hair	F	18	19	2	.11	1	.05	decrease
	Grabbing clothes	F	18	19	5	.28	1	.05	decrease
	Sliding off chair	F	18	19	10	.56	0	0	decrease
Jolly									
Ruth	Visits to toilet	F	10	22	2	.02	0	0	decrease
	Running/throwing	F	10	22	2	.02	0	0	decrease
	Obsessive play with tea towels	F	10	22	4	.04	0	0	decrease
	Bites own arm	F	10	22	2	02	0	0	decrease
Darren	Obsessive play-ing with liquids	F	9	23	2	.22	4	.17	decrease
	Hand tapping	F	9	23	14	1.5	20	.86	decrease
	Screaming	F	9	23	1	.1	8	.34	increase
	Climbing walls	F	9	23	0	0	4	.17	increase
Adam	Waving head	F	11	23	9	.8	0	0	decrease
	Hand movements	F	11	23	1	.09	27	1.7	increase
	Bites/scratches	F	11	23	1	.09	0	0	decrease
	Screams	F	11	23	34	3.1	0	0	decrease
Merry									
Alan	Head Hitting	D	46	17	41	.89	11	.64	decrease
	Crying	D	46	17	23	.50	2	.12	decrease
Pleasant									
John	Running in class	F	34	27	11	.32	1	.03	decrease
	Running out of class	F	34	27	14	.41	1	.03	decrease
	Aggression	F	34	27	11	.32	0	0	decrease

F/D = behaviour measured as frequency (F) or duration (D). Observation intervals were five minutes long.

Freq. = Total frequency for period of observation (frequency measures) or number of intervals in which behaviour was observed (duration measures).

Rate = Frequency divided by number of observation intervals (frequency measures) or percentage of observation intervals during which the behaviour occured (duration measures).

Table 7.1 (continued)

School/ pupil	Behaviour	F/D	Number of Intervals		Pre Freq. rate	Post Freq. rate		Change
			Pre	Post				
Lively								
Jack	Thumb in mouth	F	12	16	6	0.5	7	.44	increase
	Rubbing head	F	12	16	3	.25	0	0	decrease
	Slapping/tapping	F	12	16	10	.8	1	.06	decrease
	Raspberry noices	F	12	16	3	.25	2	.13	decrease
	Pushes table	F	12	16	1	.08	0	0	decrease
	Shouts	F	12	16	4	.33	0	0	decrease
	Inappropriate noises	F	12	16	7	.58	2	.12	decrease
Mick	Scratching	F	29	20	2	.06	0	0	decrease
	Non-compliance	F	29	20	5	.17	2	.01	decrease
	Running	F	29	20	0	0	3	.15	increase
	Eating plaster	F	29	20	1	.03	0	0	decrease
	Pushing	F	29	20	1	.03	0	0	decrease
Neil	Runs in/out of classroom	F	17	17	4	.23	6	.35	increase
	Whines/screams	F	17	17	6	.35	2	.11	decrease
	Interferes with others	F	17	17	16	.94	7	.41	decrease
	Non-compliance	F	17	17	4	.23	4	.23	no change
Cheerful								
Chris	Pinching	F	47	9	3	.06	0	0	decrease
	Throwing	F	47	9	9	.19	0	0	decrease
	Kicking floor	F	47	9	11	.23	0	0	decrease
	Dropping to knees	F	47	9	21	.44	0	0	decrease
Bright								
Colin	Running in class	F	70	13	16	23	7	.54	increase
	Aggression	F	70	13	2	.03	0	0	decrease
Harry	Shouting	F	82	22	35	.43	9	.41	decrease
	Non-compliance	F	82	22	10	.12	13	.59	increase
	Sitting on floor	F	82	22	11	.13	0	0	decrease
	Taunting/teasing	F	82	22	12	.15	5	.23	increase
Carol	Scratching/biting	F	26	25	8	.3	7	.28	decrease
	Screaming	F	26	25	5	.19	6	.24	increase
	Throwing	F	26	25	1	.04	0	0	decrease
Friendly								
Mary	Aggression	F	30	27	1	.03	1	.04	increase
	Running	F	30	27	0	0	1	.04	increase
	Shouting	F	30	27	7	.23	7	.25	increase

Behaviour change is expressed as the difference between the rate of occurrence pre- and post-intervention. In many cases, overall frequency is low and the reliability of the change measure is suspect. For example, one behaviour, unnecessary visits to the toilet, presented by Ruth, changes from .02 (i.e. one visit per four hours of observation), to zero after a period of intervention. In other cases, the changes in rate are quite marked. For example, Martin would slide off his chair approximately once every ten minutes before intervention (rate = .56). This was reduced to zero after intervention. Darren engaged in hand tapping almost constantly prior to intervention (rate = 1.5). This fell to rather less than once every five minutes after intervention (rate =.86). The reliability of these measures is considered in more detail at the end of this section.

Overall, the measures taken from observational transcripts suggest modest reductions in the majority of the challenging behaviours considered. Fifty-five behaviours presented by fifteen pupils were analysed using this approach. Of these, forty showed some reduction in the rate of occurrence after intervention. Fourteen showed an increase and one showed no change. Five pupils showed a decrease in all behaviours analysed and one (Mary) showed an increase across all three behaviours. The nine other pupils showed a mixed pattern with some behaviours decreasing in frequency of occurrence while others increased.

Results based on teacher recording
Teacher records were only completed pre- and post-intervention for pupils in Phase II schools. To facilitate comparison with the classroom observations carried out by the project staff, the total time during which recording was carried out is expressed in five minute intervals (number of teacher recording sessions x 3). Total recording time per pupil varied from 210 minutes to 390 minutes with means of 334 minutes before intervention and 269 minutes after intervention.

Two measures of change are shown in Table 7:2. First, the rate of occurrence of challenging behaviours both pre and post-intervention expressed as frequency per five minute interval. Change, following intervention, is the difference between rates of occurrence before and after intervention.

The second measure of change is the number of five minute intervals during which there was no occurrence of the target behaviour. Since the number of recording intervals varied across pupils, this is expressed as a percentage of the total number of five minute recording intervals. Change is the difference between the proportion of incident free intervals (IFI) before and after intervention.

Data are presented for thirty-five behaviours and ten pupils. The overall rate of occurrence decreased in the case of eighteen behaviours but there were increases for sixteen behaviours with one showing no change. The proportion of incident free intervals decreased in respect of twenty three behaviours but increased in the case of eleven. Two pupils (Neil and Clive) showed consistent decreases in both measures for all behaviours recorded, and one pupil (Jack) showed consistent increases across behaviours and the two measures employed.

Table 7.2
Behaviour measurement derived from teacher records

School /Pupil	Behaviour	Number of intervals		Pre			Post			Change
		Pre	Post	Fre	IFI %	Rate	Freq	IFI %	Rate	
Jolly										
Ruth	Unnecessary visits to toilet	72	75	13	33 .46	.18	23	36 .48	.31	increase decrease
	Throwing	72	75	3	63 .87	.04	7	63 .84	.09	increase increase
	Pinching	72	75	16	36 .5	.22	63	36 .48	.84	increase increase
	Kicking	72	75	1	69 .96	.01	3	72 .96	.04	increase no change
Darren	Obsessive play with liquids	75	75	9	57 .76	.12	4	63 .84	.05	decrease decrease
	Hand tapping	75	75	33	24 .32	.44	35	30 .4	.46	increase decrease
	Screaming	75	75	0	75 1.0	0	2	69 .92	.02	increase increase
	Climbing	75	75	5	66 .88	.06	5	69 .92	.06	no change decrease
Adam	Head waving	66	51	25	18 .27	.38	15	30 .59	.29	decrease decrease
	Hand movements	66	51	9	42 .64	.14	21	18 .35	.41	increase increase
	Bites/ scratches	66	51	5	54 .81	.07	5	36 .70	.1	increase increase
Joyful										
Simon	Crying	60	42	34	15 .25	.57	15	15 .36	.36	decrease decrease
	Refusal to walk	60	42	3	54 .9	.05	4	30 .71	.09	increase increase
	Pushing things away	60	42	14	39 .65	.23	24	21 .5	.57	increase increase
Martin	Throwing	72	51	7	60 .83	.09	8	24 .47	.12	increase increase
	Pulling hair	72	51	7	57 .79	.09	6	45 .88	.08	decrease decrease
	Grabbing clothes	72	51	21	39 .54	.29	4	30 .59	.23	decrease decrease
	Sliding off chair	72	51	10	45 .62	.14	12	33 .65	.16	increase decrease

Freq = Number of times each behaviour was observed and recorded.
Rate = Number of target behaviours recorded divided by number of observation intervals.
IFI (first line) = Number of observation intervals when target behaviour was not observed.
IFI (second line) = Number of incident free intervals divided by total number of observation intervals.

Table 7.2 (continued)

School/ pupil	Behaviour	Number of intervals		Pre			Post			Change
		Pre	Post	Freq	IFI %	Rate	Freq	IFI %	Rate	
Lively										
Mick	Scratching	78	57	12	57 .73	.15	0	57 1.0	0	decrease decrease
	Non-compliance	78	57	28	45 .57	.35	2	51 .89	.03	decrease decrease
	Running	78	57	4	66 .84	.05	5	54 .94	.09	increase decrease
	Eating plaster	78	57	5	72 .92	.06	0	57 1.0	0	decrease decrease
	Pushing	78	57	9	66 .84	.11	1	54 .94	.02	decrease decrease
	Slapping/ Tapping	72	75	16	45 .62	.22	56	9 .12	.74	increase increase
	Noises	72	75	12	54 .75	.16	66	18 .24	.88	increase increase
	Runs away	57	54	12	30 .52	.21	3	48 .88	.05	decrease decrease
Neil	Whining/ screaming	57	54	15	27 .47	.26	4	42 .77	.07	decrease decrease
	Pushes away from table/non compliance	57	57	19	27 .47	.33	9	42 .77	.16	decrease decrease
Cheerful										
Clive	Flapping	69	51	114	3 .04	1.6	17	21 .41	.33	decrease decrease
	Nail digging	69	51	122	6 .08	1.7	0	51 1.0	0	decrease decrease
	Screaming	69	51	20	45 .65	.29	0	51 1.0	0	decrease decrease
	Stamping	69	51	12	57 .83	.17	0	51 1.0	0	decrease decrease
Chris	Pinching	48	48	13	11 .23	.27	0	48 1.0	0	decrease decrease
	Throwing	48	48	5	42 .87	.11	1	45 1.0	.02	decrease decrease
	Licking	48	48	28	15 31	.58	50	3 .06	1.0	increase increase

It is usual practice to establish the reliability of any observational measure by arranging for simultaneous recording of a sample of behaviours by two people working independently. Direct comparison of overall measures of frequency or of the categories assigned to specific events provides the basis for a measure of inter-rater agreement. In this study, limited resources and a flexible approach to the selection of recording intervals by classroom staff made this approach impractical. Instead, reliability is evaluated in respect of the measures derived from classroom observations by the project staff and teacher recordings of problem behaviour. This approach to reliability is only possible where both methods of data collection address identical behaviours.

The data for the twenty-four behaviours for which comparable data were available from observation by project staff and teacher recording are shown in Table 7:3 If overall frequencies are compared, rates of occurrence decrease on both measures for thirteen behaviours and increase on both measures in respect of four behaviours. Direction of change differs in the case of ten behaviours. If the incident free interval (IFI) measure is employed from the teacher recorded data, there is agreement on seventeen behaviours (three counts of behaviours which increase and fourteen behaviours which decrease) and disagreement arising from eight behaviours.

A measure of reliability can be derived by comparing the agreements on the direction of change over time with disagreements. For the frequency data this is 60% and for the incident free interval data 68%. It should be noted that when using direction of change as a basis for comparison, a level of 50% agreement between the measures could be expected to occur by chance alone. Thus, while the comparison of results from the two sets of data supports the conclusion that interventions resulted in generally positive outcomes, only a modest level of measurement reliability has been established.

On the other hand, quite different approaches to data collection and analysis were employed in generating these two data sets, and there was no opportunity to agree on time samples for observation; in most cases, the two sets of data were obtained from observations at different times and often on different days. Low agreement therefore reflects variation in the actual occurrence of the behaviours under consideration, as well as bias arising from the methodology employed and observer error. Furthermore, total time available for the observation of each pupil was highly variable and, in some cases, extremely short. Under these circumstances, it may be argued that the measures employed provide reasonably robust evidence about behaviour change following the period of intervention.

Table 7.3

Agreements between measures of change derived from observations by project staff and teacher recording

School/Pupil	Behaviour	Direction of Change			Agreement	
		Project	Teachers			
		Observation	Recording Frequency	Recording IFI	Freq	IFI
Jolly						
Ruth	Visits to toilet	dec	inc	dec	D	A
Darren	Obsessive play with liquids	dec	dec	dec	A	A
	Hand tapping	dec	inc	dec	D	A
	Screaming	inc	inc	inc	A	A
	Climbing	inc	n/c	dec	D	D
Adam	Hand waving	dec	dec	dec	A	A
	Hand movements	inc	inc	inc	A	A
	Bites/scratches	dec	inc	inc	D	D
Joyful						
Martin	Throwing	inc	inc	inc	A	A
	Pulling hair	dec	dec	dec	A	A
	Grabbing clothes	dec	dec	dec	A	A
	Sliding off chair	dec	inc	dec	D	A
Lively						
Mick	Scratching	dec	dec	dec	A	A
	Non-compliance	dec	dec	dec	A	A
	Running	inc	inc	dec	A	D
	Eating plaster	dec	dec	dec	A	A
	Pinching	dec	dec	dec	A	A
Jack	Slapping/tapping	dec	inc	inc	D	D
	Noises	dec	inc	inc	D	D
Neil	Running away	inc	dec	dec	D	D
	Whinig/ screaming	dec	dec	dec	A	A
	Pushing away from table	N/C	dec	dec	D	D
Cheerful						
Chris	Pinching	dec	dec	dec	A	A
	Throwing	dec	dec	dec	A	A
	Licking	dec	inc	inc	D	D

Summary

In the second part of this chapter, we have described two procedures for collecting observational data from the behaviour of pupils before and after they received the interventions which were agreed at the review meetings. As part of the 'shadowing' exercise, a member of the project team made notes on classroom activities and the behaviour of the targeted pupils. Pre-and post-intervention records were available for sixteen pupils. Teachers of those pupils who were selected for direct involvement in the project were also asked to make classroom records of challenging behaviours. Unfortunately, teachers in Phase I schools experienced considerable difficulty in providing systematic records both before and after the interventions were introduced. However, following participation in an additional workshop on record keeping organised by members of the project team, most of the teachers in Phase II schools provided observational data which could be used to assess the impact of the intervention.

The data presented in this chapter indicate modest reductions in many challenging behaviours and support the conclusion that the interventions have direct impact on the frequency or duration of the challenging behaviours presented by pupils. However, it is also clear that both measures lacked technical sophistication and it was not possible to establish the level of inter-rater reliability of the data collected by teachers or the project staff using conventional methods. Furthermore, the new methods of working with pupils had only been introduced for a relatively brief period before the post intervention records were made. For these reasons, the data need to be interpreted with caution.

The evidence presented in this chapter suggests that teachers need to develop skills and classroom procedures which facilitate systematic recording of challenging behaviours in the classroom. Accurate records are essential if intervention strategies are to be properly evaluated, and observation and data collection should be regarded as integral components of any school-based strategy which sets out to address the needs of pupils with challenging behaviours.

Learning Resources
Centre

Chapter 8

RESULTS OF THE POST INTERVENTION EVALUATION

After a period of between eight and nine months in the case of Phase I schools (including the summer holiday) and between five and six months in the case of Phase II schools, the consultancy support was withdrawn and a number of evaluation questionnaires were distributed to teachers, head teachers and classroom support workers. The main areas explored were as follows:

- Overall satisfaction with the conduct of the project: feedback from teachers, head teachers and classroom support workers.

- Perceived efficacy of the project: feedback from classroom teachers.

- Integrating good practice: teachers' perception of strategies for addressing challenging behaviour.

Throughout the project, intervention was established through collaboration with the staff of the schools concerned. One of the objectives of the evaluation was to determine how successful this approach had been. The 'satisfaction questionnaire' invited respondents to indicate their level of satisfaction with each component of the project (see Chapter 5 for a review of these components) and the associated outcomes.

The second broad area of interest is the extent to which teachers perceive the project as having made a difference to their own methods of working and, as a consequence, to the pupils concerned. Perceived efficacy must, of course, be separated from other more objective measures of outcome. However, unless the project has face validity for those who were directly involved and ultimately responsible for implementation, it is unlikely to be a viable approach to school-based interventions.

The third area of evaluation was concerned with the social validity of the different strategies designed to reduce or ameliorate challenging behaviours (Wolf, 1978). As already indicated in Chapter 2, we were particularly concerned with developing strategies which would be acceptable to teachers and would work in schools. In the final questionnaire we asked specific questions about how successfully strategies had been agreed and implemented and whether the respondents saw them as viable methods of working with pupils who presented challenging behaviours after the project had finished. Examples of all three questionnaires used in this part of the project evaluation are included in Appendix 1.

Table 8.1
Results of project evaluation: Teacher's satisfaction ratings

Figures show number 'very satisfied' or 'satisfied'
(Figures in parenthesis indicate missing data)

How satisfied are you with:	Teachers		Support Workers		Head Teachers	
	Phase I N=13	Phase II N=10	Phase I N=6	Phase II N=8	Phase I N=5	Phase II N=1
Whole school meetings at start of project	10	8	2(1)	7	5	1
Way in which pupils were selected	10	8	4(1)	7	4	1
The interview (used in Phase I only)	9(1)					
The self report questionnaire (Phase II only)		6				
'Shadowing' by project staff	11	8	4	5	4	1
Training on observation (Phase II only)		6		8		
Involvement in record keeping	6	5	2	7	1(2)	1
Review meetings	6	6	2	8	5	1
Outcome of review meetings	8	5	2	6	4	1
The intervention programme	7	8	3	5	5	1
Support from project team	5(1)	9	3	5	5	1
Support from head teacher (teachers)	3(1)	3(2)				
Involvement of parents	1(3)	0(1)	0	0	0	0
Positive outcomes for selective pupils	9	4	2	5	4	0
Positive outcomes for other pupils	6(1)	1	2	2	3	0
Positive outcomes for school as a whole	4	1	2	3	5	1

Satisfaction with the project methodology

Table 8.1 shows the number of teachers, head teachers and classroom support workers who indicated that they were satisfied or very satisfied with the different components of the project when asked to note their satisfaction on a five point scale (very satisfied through to very dissatisfied). Apart from the classroom support workers in Phase I, most of the staff were satisfied with the conduct of the whole school meetings, the selection of pupils and the classroom observation (shadowing) carried out by the project staff. About 70% of the teachers were satisfied with the semi-structured interview (Phase I) and this figure did not change with the introduction of the self-report questionnaire.

The proportion of teachers satisfied with their involvement in recording challenging behaviours did not change from about 50% between Phase I and Phase II even though a training session was provided for staff in Phase II. Only 60% of teachers expressed satisfaction with this training, while all eight classroom support workers were satisfied. Comments indicate some of the difficulties faced by staff when trying to record behaviours in the classroom

- 'Very frustrating because I wanted to be able to record but found it very difficult to keep track of all behaviours and what was required'. (Phase I teacher)

- 'I needed to be much more organised'. (Phase I teacher)

- 'Too time consuming' (Phase I teacher)

- 'Too much to do in one day; difficult to find time' (Phase II teacher)

- Time factor and other educational demands restricted the degree of accuracy, also the speed at which things happened and my being distracted by other children/adults' (Phase II teacher).

The outcome of review meetings were regarded as successful by slightly more teachers in Phase I schools than Phase II schools. In contrast, more classroom support workers in Phase II than Phase I rated them as satisfactory. One teacher in Phase I said 'I was left feeling despondent and wondering how I was going to get it all done'. Another commented, 'The objectives and help given were extremely useful but I have found much difficulty in continuing to implement, for example, finding appropriate activities for a structured day'. One Phase II teacher expressed concern about finding cover for her classroom support workers.

The intervention programme and support from the project team was regarded as more satisfactory by staff in Phase II compared to those in Phase 1. This may be a result of the developmental transfer of good practice by the project team. One teacher in Phase I said, 'I don't feel I've had any support; just been asked to observe and try things out that I would have had to come up with anyway'. Another in Phase II said, 'Whilst we tried to carry out the intervention programme, we felt we needed some more guidance and ideas that were practical'. These comments point to the complexity of working with teachers with differing levels of expertise and pupils with highly complex needs.

When discussing the role of head teachers (principals) in school development, Fullan (1991) comments 'While the Principal strongly influences the likelihood of change, most Principals do not play instructional or change leadership roles... Change projects that have the active support of Principals are more likely to succeed' (p.76). In this study, the majority of teachers who completed this questionnaire regarded the support from their head teachers as unsatisfactory. Phase I teachers from different schools commented:

- 'There has been no involvement by the head teacher. The planning of the intervention programme was wholly the responsibility of the class teacher and there have been no queries as to its content or successful outcome.'

- 'Little support given.'

- 'Haven't had any.'

Phase II teachers, all from different schools, said:

- 'At the outset, the head seemed very keen on the programme. However, when it came to providing cover, the keenness to help evaporated.'

- 'No support given at all.'

- 'No noticeable support after initial whole school meeting and meeting to select pupils.'

The satisfaction with involvement of classroom support workers and other staff was variable ranging from 90% for support workers in Phase II to as low as 25% from other teachers in Phase I.

Some of the classroom support workers in Phase I schools expressed their concern about their lack of involvement in the intervention process:

- 'I was not involved in many of the meetings; only the teacher.'

- 'I felt that I was not wholly involved... I feel that the principles behind this are really good, but I feel that there has to be more team work; it can't work if we don't all know what's going on.'

During the project, there was insufficient time and limited resources for encouraging the practical involvement of parents. Nevertheless, we felt it was important to include a question about collaboration with parents. Understandably, there was little satisfaction with the way in which parents were involved. As one teacher put it, 'What involvement?'

There was some variability regarding the expressed satisfaction for outcomes in relation to pupils with challenging behaviour, their peers and the school as a whole. Rather more teachers in Phase I compared to Phase II felt satisfied with these areas; for classroom support workers this pattern was reversed with greater satisfaction expressed by those in Phase II. More teachers and classroom support workers were satisfied with the outcomes for the selected pupils than were satisfied with outcomes for other pupils or the school as a whole. This probably reflects the pattern of working during the project, which deliberately focused on the needs of individual pupils before looking at the implications within the classroom and the school, of proposed intervention strategies.

Perceived efficacy of the project

The evaluation questionnaire on perceived efficacy provided information on the extent to which teachers implemented three broad strategies: reactive strategies for responding to instances of challenging behaviours; proactive strategies to reduce challenging behaviours; teaching new skills.

Questions about pupil behaviours focused on involvement in group activities and interactions with teachers, classroom support workers, and other pupils. These data are summarised in Table 8.2.

This part of the questionnaire was completed in respect of the impact of the project on individual pupils. In one school, two pupils were transferred to a different class during the course of the project. Both the original teachers and the teacher of the new class was asked to complete this part of the questionnaire. This produced an increase in the number of respondents from 13 to 15. Overall, new responses were reported in respect of 25 teachers who worked with pupils directly involved in the project.

Fourteen teachers thought that the new approach was more effective than strategies they had previously employed. Nineteen teachers indicated that they had adopted new strategies for reducing the likelihood of challenging behaviour. Positive consequences were identified in respect of lower frequencies (10) less intense behaviours (9) and behaviours of shorter duration (8), although six teachers also noted new forms of challenging behaviour emerging.

There was little evidence of changes in behaviour when pupils were with other staff: six teachers noted lower frequencies, four commented on lower intensity behaviour and three thought that behaviours were of shorter duration. New forms of challenging behaviour were identified by four teachers.

Table 8.2

Results of project evaluation: Teachers' perception of efficacy

(Teachers responded for EACH child in project. Figures in parentheses indicate missing data)

	Phase I N = 15*	Phase II N = 10
Did the project lead to:		
Changed response to challenging behaviour by teachers	12	5(5)
Number saying Yes		
Response is rated:		
More effective	11	3
Less effective	0	0
No difference	1	2
New strategies for prevention of challenging behaviour introduced		
Number saying Yes	13(1)	6(2)
Resultant changes in pupils' behaviour:		
Increase in challenging behaviour	0	0
No change in challenging behaviour	3	
Lower frequency of challenging behaviour	7	3
Less intense challenging behaviour	5	4
Shorter duration challenging behaviour	6	2
New forms of challenging behaviour	5	1
Missing	(2)	(4)
Changes in challenging behaviour when pupil is with other staff		
Number saying 'Yes'		
Increase in challenging behaviour	3	2
No change in challenging behaviour	2	5
Less frequency challenging behaviour	5	1
Less intense challenging behaviour	2	1
Shorter duration challenging behaviour	1	0
Other new forms of challenging behaviour	3	1
Missing	(1)	
Any new approaches to help pupils to learn new skills?		
Number saying 'Yes'	11	7
Outcome: Not successful	0	0
Somewhat successful	7	6
Very successful	3	1
Missing	(5)	(3)
Have new skills made any difference to the management of pupil?		
Number saying 'Yes'	6(4)	2(5)

Table 8.2 (continued)

	Phase I N = 15*	Phase II N = 10
Changes in pupil's participation in group work Number saying 'Yes'		
No change	9	5
Participates less	2	0
Participates more	3	4
Missing	(1)	(1)
Changes in interactions with other pupils Number saying 'Yes'		
Increase in positive interactions	5	0
Increase in negative interactions	0	0
Reduction in positive interactions	0	0
Reduction in negative interactions	1	1
No change	8	9
Missing	(1)	
Changes in teacher's interactions with pupil Number saying 'Yes'		
Increase in positive interactions	9	7
Increase in negative interactions	0	0
Reduction in positive interactions	0	0
Reduction in negative interactions	3	2
No change	2	2
Missing	(1)	
Changes in pupil's interactions with classroom support Number saying 'Yes'		
Increase in positive interactions	9	5
Increase in negative interactions	0	0
Reduction in positive interactions	0	0
Reduction in negative interactions	1	3
No change	4	3
Missing	(1)	
Changes in pupil's interaction with other teachers Number saying 'Yes'		
Increase in positive interactions**	7	1
Increase in negative interactions	0	0
Reduction in positive interactions	1	0
Reduction in negative interactions**	1	1
No change	7	8
Missing	(1)	

*N = 15: two pupils changed class during the project; both the original class teacher and the new class teacher responded to the questions on the effectiveness of the interventions employed with these two pupils.
**one respondent included both changes

The development of new skills was attempted by eighteen teachers and this was considered to be very successful or somewhat successful by seventeen respondents. Eight teachers thought the new skills made a difference to managing the problem behaviours.

Turning to the dependent measures of pupil behaviour following the introduction of these strategies, seven teachers thought the pupils participated in groups more often, five saw an increase in positive interactions with other pupils but only two thought that negative interactions with their peers had been reduced.

Increased positive interactions with pupils were reported by sixteen teachers. Fourteen felt that there were more positive interactions between the pupil and classroom assistants. There was a reduction in negative interactions between pupils and their teachers in the case of five children and reduced negative interactions with classroom support workers were reported for only four pupils. Changes in interactions with other teachers were less marked with only eight reports of increased positive interactions and two reductions in negative interactions.

Integrating Good Practice: teachers' perception of strategies for addressing challenging behaviour

The third section of the evaluation questionnaire invited the teachers who participated in the project to comment on the process by which new strategies were agreed and implemented. They were also asked whether they felt confident in their own ability to develop and implement similar strategies. They were invited to comment on the support they received from their own classroom support workers and from other teachers. Finally, they were asked whether they felt the project had been successful in establishing a whole school strategy and how confident they were that it would be maintained. Some questions included a five point rating scale which invited respondents to indicate how confident they were in their ability to carry forward the work developed during the project. The scale points ranged from *very confident* to *not at all confident*. The results are summarised in Table 8.3.

At the end of the project, eighteen out of twenty-three teachers who completed the questionnaire felt confident in their ability to identify challenging behaviours. Ten teachers said their views on challenging behaviour had changed as a result of the project and eight thought that they had been helped to recognise challenging behaviours. Eleven teachers reported making a record of challenging behaviour during the project and twenty-one were quite confident that they could make their own record of challenging behaviours, although only seven had actually done so.

Table 8.3
Results of project evaluation
Teachers' perceptions of their ability to carry forward the project work

(Figures in parentheses indicate missing data)

	Phase I N = 13	Phase II N = 10
Identification of challenging behaviours		
Changed views on challenging behaviours Number saying 'Yes'	7	3
Project helped with identification of challenging behaviours Number saying 'Yes'	3	5
Following project, confident in ability to identify challenging behaviours Number saying 'Yes'	9(1)	9
Made an accurate record of challenging behaviours during project Number saying 'Yes'	5	6
Foolowing project could make own record of challenging behaviours Very confident or quite confident:	12	9
Have made record since project finished Number saying 'Yes'	3	4
Strategies for responding to challenging behaviours		
During project agreed on strategies Number saying 'Yes'	11	9
Confidence in own ability Very confident or quite confident	12	10
Has developed own strategy since project finished Number saying 'Yes'	9(1)	5(1)
During project implemented strategies Number saying 'Yes'	10	9
Confidence in implementing own strategies: Very confident or quite confident	12	10
Has implemented own strategies since project finished Number saying 'Yes'	9(1)	6(2)
Strategies for reducing occurrence of challenging behaviours		
During project agreed on strategies Number saying 'Yes'	11	8(2)
Confidence in own ability Very confident or quite confident	11	10

Table 8.3 (continued)

	Phase I N = 13	Phase II N = 10
Has developed own strategy Number saying 'Yes'	3(4)	4(2)
During project implemented strategies Number saying 'Yes'	4	4
Confidence in implementing own strategies Very confident or quite confident	11	10
Has implemented strategies since project finished Number saying 'Yes'	4(3)	3(2)
Strategies for teaching new skills		
During project agreed on strategies Number saying 'Yes'	7(1)	7
Confidence in own ability Very confident or quite confident	11	9
Has developed own strategy Number saying 'Yes'	3(4)	2(2)
During project implemented strategies Number saying 'Yes'	7(1)	4
Confidence in implementing own strategies Very confident or quite confident	11	9
Has implemented strategy since project finished Number saying 'Yes'	5(2)	2(3)
Strategies for involving pupil in group activities		
During project agreed strategies Number saying 'Yes'	9(1)	5
Confidence in own ability Very confident or quite confident	10	7
Has developed strategy Number saying 'Yes'	6(3)	3(3)
During project implemented strategies Number saying 'Yes'	9	4(1)
Confidence in own ability Very confident or quite confident	11	7(1)
Has implemented strategy since project finished Number saying 'Yes'	5(2)	4(3)

Twenty-two of the teachers were *quite* confident or *very* confident of their own ability to develop and implement a strategy to respond to challenging behaviours, but only fourteen said they had done so after the completion of the project. Twenty teachers reported agreeing strategies for responding to incidents of challenging behaviours during the project and nineteen said that these had been implemented. Similar numbers of teachers expressed confidence in their ability to develop and implement strategies for reducing the likelihood of challenging behaviour, although fewer than seven had actually done so. Nineteen teachers said they agreed preventative strategies during the project, but only eight had implemented them.

Twenty teachers felt *quite* confident or *very* confident in their ability to develop and implement a strategy for helping a pupil with challenging behaviour to learn new skills. During the project, fourteen teachers had agreed on this type of strategy and eleven indicated that they were able to implement it. Only seven teachers said they had actually implemented this kind of strategy since the project had finished.

Slightly fewer teachers felt confident in their ability to develop and implement new strategies for involving pupils in group activities (seventeen and eighteen respectively). Although fourteen had agreed strategies to achieve this, and thirteen had introduced this type of strategy during the project, only nine had done so subsequently.

Overall, there is substantial evidence that teachers feel comfortable with these strategies for responding to pupils with challenging behaviour and confident of their ability both to develop and implement similar strategies to meet the needs of other pupils. Evidence in support of these views, for example, in terms of independent action to develop and implement strategies following the withdrawal of consultancy support, is somewhat weaker. This may be partly due to the relatively short interval which had elapsed between the end of the project and the completion of the questionnaires. However, it does suggest that the confidence expressed by teachers in applying new strategies should be treated cautiously until there is concrete evidence that new styles of working have been successfully introduced in the absence of external consultancy support.

Introducing change in schools involves effective collaboration among colleagues. 'School improvements are most likely when teachers engage in continuous and increasingly concrete and precise talk about teaching practice' (Fullan, p.77). We asked teachers to comment on whether they were able to work successfully with their classroom support staff and their colleagues (Table 8.4).

At least 70% of teachers thought that they had been able to work successfully with the classroom support staff during the project, while 63% or more expressed the view that they had worked successfully with other teachers in the school. At the end of the project, 80% expressed confidence in their ability to continue working closely with the classroom support staff in the five main stages of the intervention process. Nearly 70% of respondents were also confident of their ability to carry on working successfully with their teacher colleagues.

Table 8.4
Results of project evaluation
Teachers working in collaboration with other staff
(Figures in parenthesis indicate missing data)

	Teachers working with support workers		Teachers working with other teachers	
	Phase I N=13	Phase II N=10	Phase I N=13	Phase II N=10
Collaboration during the project in the following areas:				
Identification of pupils Number saying 'Yes'	11(1)	9	12	8(1)
Identification of challenging behaviours	10(1)	10	12	8(1)
Recording challenging behaviours	8	9	7(1)	8(1)
Developing strategies	9	9	8(1)	6(2)
Implementing strategies	10(1)	10	8(2)	6(2)
Collaboration after the project in the following areas: (Numbers indicating 'confident' or 'quite confident')				
Identifying pupils	12(1)	9	13	8(2)
Identifying challenging behaviour	12(1)	10	13	7(3)
Recording challenging behaviours	10(2)	9	10(1)	7(2)
Developing strategies	11(1)	9	13	9(2)
Implementing strategies	11(1)	10	10(2)	6(3)

The efficacy of a whole school approach was addressed through two questions concerned with what had happened during the project and what the teachers felt was likely to happen subsequently. Comparative data from the head teachers' questionnaire is included in Table 8.5. Whereas only ten of the twenty-three teachers felt the whole school approach had been successful or moderately successful, all six of the head teachers who responded expressed this view. Similarly, only half of the teachers felt optimistic about the maintenance of a whole school approach while all six heads were confident or quite confident. This suggests a considerable difference in the way in which teachers and head teachers viewed the impact of the project and, in itself, raises questions about the future development of the methods and ideas which we sought to establish.

Table 8.5
Results of Project Evaluation: perceived efficacy of a whole school approach

| | Teachers | | Head teachers | |
	Phase I N = 13	Phase II N = 10	Phase I N = 5	Phase II N = 1
Successful or moderately successful during the project	6(1)	4	5	1
Confident or quite confident that it will be maintained	7	5	5	1

Two questions were included which invited respondents to take a broader and longer term view of the project. First, we asked teachers and head teachers to comment on the single most important outcome from their involvement in the project and, secondly, to state what still needed to be done in their schools to ensure that pupils with challenging behaviours received appropriate help.

Most important outcomes
The comments about the most important outcome were varied, indicating the complex range of skills and abilities which are required to work effectively with pupils who challenge. However, two clear themes do emerge. First, many comments reflected teachers' concerns about their own competencies and the importance of being able to share personal and professional concerns with another experienced co-worker who understood the special demands made upon good professional practice by pupils who present challenging behaviours:

- 'Confirmation of strengths from an experienced teacher from outside the school ... Empathy and positive counselling in implementing class strategies and management of staff.'

- 'The chance to discuss the child's challenging behaviour with someone who could view it positively rather than negatively, therefore giving hope of a successful outcome eventually.'

- 'Talking to someone, and being able to look at things from a new angle and take myself out of the situation emotionally.'

- 'Recognition of the fact that these children aren't just naughty/disruptive, but have very specific needs which can be met.'

- 'That I am not alone in my philosophy regarding the education of SLD pupils.'

- 'Confirmation that we are on the right track with this pupil.'

A number of teachers specifically referred to their sense of increased confidence arising from this process of support and consultation:

- 'It has stopped one child from dominating the whole class, and has given me the confidence to tackle other challenging behaviours.'

- 'We feel confident that what we have been doing is correct. It has increased our confidence as a staff.'

- 'Feel more confident in ability to deal with challenging behaviour.'

A comment from one head teacher echoed the importance of dialogue with an experienced professional:

- 'A chance to talk over what are seemingly unsolvable problems and to hear a more expert point of view from someone who is willing to listen.'

Secondly, both teachers and head teachers referred to specific skills or strategies which they had found useful:

- 'Increased my desire to learn more and increase my skills.'

- 'The structured development of strategies for interventions.'

- 'Better understanding. Awareness of change in self-attitudes, responses and organisation, etc.'

- 'Being offered a tool with which effectively to record, monitor and count specific instances of behaviour.'

- 'Ability to identify challenging behaviour in pupils.'

- 'Acquiring a method of looking at such behaviour, for example, seeing the world through the eyes of the child.'

- 'Establishing good practice and a depersonalised approach to meeting the challenge.'

- 'The staff training element.'

What still needs to be done to meet the needs of pupils with challenging behaviour in your school?

The most obvious concern for the future was the need to maintain and develop systems for staff support:

- 'A greater understanding of the need for individual staff support in order for these staff effectively to implement any strategies.'

- 'Staff (teachers and support staff) need to meet more frequently in order to discuss problems and any strategies which are developed must be carried on when a child moves into another class.'

- 'We need time and a support network for people to talk and remove the pressure.'

- 'The continuous support and acknowledgement that these children are forever demanding.'

- 'Greater communication between departments and staff...

- 'To share all experiences and suggestions.'

- 'Continued meetings by all staff.'

Some responses specifically referred to staff training:

- 'Courses for all staff.'

- 'Training for non-teaching staff.'

- 'A reinforcement of the (project) staff training.'

For others, the concept of a Whole School Approach was integral to making progress. It is not clear whether these comments reflected frustration with the lack of progress during the project or whether they were an enthusiastic endorsement of new styles of working which had already proved successful:

- 'Development of a whole school approach and in-service training.'

- 'More school approaches ... reorganisation of school groups.'

- 'More whole school support.'

- 'Increase in whole school strategies.'

- 'More whole school discussions on individual pupils and hence a whole school awareness, including staff such as dinner supervisors.'

- 'Continue to raise awareness of whole school approach and not go off the boil.'

- 'Improvement of whole school approach.'

- 'More effective and consistent whole school approach.'

- 'We need to develop a whole school policy with set down guidelines and an understanding from all staff.'

- 'Whole school policy.'

Inevitably, some respondents emphasised the need for additional resources to facilitate new approaches and methods of working:

- 'Need the resources to be able to continue to offer children/students curriculum experiences appropriate to their needs.'

- 'Increased resourcing (personnel).'

- 'More resources: financial/staffing from local education authority.'

Interestingly, these last comments were made by classroom staff and not by head teachers.

Final comments
At the end of the questionnaire, all respondents were invited to make any other comments about the project. A number of positive comments were made including support for the general approach adopted and expressions of appreciation for the personal commitment and support offered by the project officer:

- 'The project was very successful from my point of view and the project team were a pleasure to work with.'

- 'I really enjoyed being involved in the project and found it interesting and informative.'

- 'The support and help was valuable and much appreciated.'

- 'Thank you for your time, your insight and your never ceasing support.'

- 'We found the input most valuable (the project team were) unobtrusive and yet always available to listen and give experience. An extremely valuable project.'

There were also comments about the time and effort required from staff working directly with the pupils involved in the project:

- 'Although the time taken was often lengthy, it did enable me to take a more objective view of situations and behaviours.'

- 'I found the project useful but time consuming.'

- 'Whilst my involvement in the project was time consuming, this was more than compensated for by the enjoyment of participating in such a well organised exercise and the worthwhile discussion and intervention programme.'

However, two teachers felt that the questionnaire had not explored the impact of the project in sufficient detail. They expressed reservations regarding the extent to which specific interventions were introduced as a direct result of the involvement of the project team and also questioned whether improvements in pupil behaviour could be directly linked to the new methods of working agreed at the Review Meetings:

- 'I think that in the case of N, the project wasn't the factor that initiated his dramatic improvement. The main strategy of using communication was first suggested by the Educational Psychologist, but I felt that the project helped in refining the strategy.'

- 'Difficult to assess how much the improvement in the pupil is attributed to involvement in the project or whether the staff adjusting to the needs of the pupil and vice versa produced improvement.'

Clearly, both of these comments make important points which underline our general strategy of collaborating with teachers and support workers and trying to establish interventions which fit within a particular school or classroom. The question of what precise changes are responsible for improvements (or a deterioration) in a pupil's behaviour are always going to invite complex and unsatisfactory answers. Rather than seeking to identify a single cause or factor which can lead to positive outcomes, we have, instead, sought to ask what it is, about this pupil's life in school, which makes challenging behaviour more likely to occur. And, conversely, what changes can be introduced within the school and the classroom which will reduce the likelihood of those behaviours occurring. Such a strategy is based upon stacking the odds against challenging behaviours and doing everything possible to encourage appropriate or positive behaviours. In such circumstances, it makes little sense to debate whether staff consistency, the increased range of curriculum options or the opportunity to 'opt out' of group sessions, was the key factor which caused the changed behaviour.

We end this section with a comment which makes oblique reference to the wider context of education. It is a timely reminder of the limited scope of the project and of the need for further work to ensure that schools and families receive appropriate help:

- 'I hope that as a result of this research a whole school policy will be developed which incorporates parental involvement to a greater degree and recognition of these children's specific needs by Education Authorities and government at national level.'

Summary
The post intervention questionnaire was designed to explore the success of the project from the perspective of those whom we have described as 'collaborators' or 'co-workers'. Staff were asked to evaluate each aspect of the project in relation to three central questions. First, we wanted to know whether we had been successful in establishing interventions which meshed with school organisation and classroom practice; had we been able to initiate change without provoking hostility or rejection; was our style of collaborative working and one which teachers, head teachers and classroom support workers found easy to adopt as part of their own everyday practice?

Satisfaction
While the overall impression is one of staff satisfaction with the way in which the project was carried out, there are important aspects of the Whole School Approach which were rated as less than completely successful. Involvement of teachers in classroom recording was only regarded as satisfactory by about 50% of teachers and support workers even when additional training input was provided in Phase II schools. Support from the head teacher and from other teaching staff was rated satisfactory by less than 50% of those who completed questionnaires. In earlier chapters, we have emphasised the importance of gathering objective information about the frequency and duration of challenging behaviours for the development and evaluation of intervention strategies. We have also referred to the literature on school change programmes in general and noted how crucial is the role of the head teacher in carrying forward innovative new programmes. The relatively low ratings accorded to these two aspects of the project methodology are therefore likely to have had a significant impact on the outcome of this study. They also have implications for further school-based work designed to help teachers in special schools working with other pupils who present a challenge.

Teacher involvement in recording classroom behaviours raises three issues. First, teachers have little time to devote to recording and are constantly having to respond to new and unexpected events which divert their time and attention from the task of recording. Secondly, most teachers have not been trained to observe and record individual behaviours; instead, their professional skills are founded on their ability to make sense of the child as a person. For example, one teacher, 'wanted to be able to record' but, 'found it very difficult to keep track of all behaviours'. Thirdly, the rationale for recording incidents as they occur is based upon an acceptance of the fallibility of *ad hoc* judgments even when these are based on long experience. A belief in the necessity of recording implies recognition of the fact that many other professional judgments are made on the basis of flawed or inadequate information. Each of these concerns must be addressed by anyone who remains committed to the concept of collaborative research and seeks to involve teachers in data collection.

At an intuitive level, the extent to which head teachers are willing and able to provide active support and encouragement for a school project became evident at a fairly early stage. In some schools, less than wholehearted commitment by head teachers was suggested by an inability to attend Review Meetings and, in some cases, by the evident surprise when project staff arrived for a meeting which had been planned and confirmed only days previously. In other schools, the limitations of senior managers were less evident but equally detrimental to the success of the project. For example, in one school, the head was apparently unable to resolve long term personal differences between a teacher and her two support workers; in another school, the head had been unable to make any practical suggestions regarding the organisation and management of a class of six pupils, all of whom presented challenging behaviours, or to provide any form of support for the class teacher. In both schools, these unresolved management issues created a working environment in which obstacles to change were well established.

Following the Review Meetings, the extent to which head teachers were willing and able to provide practical assistance for specific approaches for working with individual pupils provided further evidence of their commitment to the project. One teacher commented, 'There has been no involvement by the head teacher. The planning of the intervention programme was wholly the responsibility of the class teacher and there have been no queries as to its content or successful outcomes'. While it was quite clear that many head teachers had little personal experience of working directly with pupils who presented a challenge and might not, therefore, have felt confident in offering advice about specific strategies, there is little doubt that many teachers felt that they had been encouraged to participate in a very demanding project and then deserted by the very people who had been responsible for its introduction in the school in the first place.

While it is important not to overlook the considerable disadvantage experienced by staff who did not feel that their work on the project enjoyed the full support of the head teacher, this was not in itself terminal; many teachers and support workers made great progress with little obvious support from their senior colleagues. It is also important to recognise that a number of the head teachers were a continuous source encouragement and practical support throughout the project.

The positive commitment of head teachers to the project was expressed in many different ways. Those areas which seemed to have most impact on the success of the project are summarised below.

1. Endorsement of a Whole School Approach to working with pupils who present a challenge. Expressing a commitment to change and a belief in improved out comes.

2. Visible and practical involvement through meetings, liaison with project staff and monitoring of staff. Maintaining involvement throughout the intervention process.

3. Facilitation: arranging cover in order that all classroom staff could attend Review Meetings and subsequent meetings to plan and review interventions; ensuring that support was available to implement agreed interventions, especially where these had implications for the school as a whole.

4. Providing staff with encouragement and, where appropriate, emotional support.

The ability to offer specific advice on different methods of working with pupils who presented a challenge was neither a necessary or a particularly desirable part of the support which could be provided by head teachers.

Effectiveness
Our second major concern in carrying out the evaluation was to ask whether teachers felt the interventions had been effective. We explored this topic for two reasons: first, teachers' perceptions can provide additional information which may endorse or refute the evidence from direct recordings and, secondly, as far as school-based interventions are concerned, there is very little advantage in developing highly effective intervention strategies if teachers don't believe that they make any difference.

The belief that interventions are effective is almost certainly necessary if teachers are to employ them on a long term basis. We were concerned with teachers' views of both the specific interventions introduced for individual pupils and the process by which schools were engaged with the task of developing and implementing intervention strategies. The majority of the teachers involved in the study said that they had changed the way in which they responded to pupils who presented a challenge, and also introduced strategies to reduce the occurrence of difficult behaviour. Most of these felt that the new methods of working produced positive effects on the challenging behaviour itself, helped pupils to learn new skills and resulted in greater participation in group work.

While there is good evidence that teachers saw the project as having a direct and positive impact on their own practice and that of their classroom support workers, they were far less optimistic about its impact on other members of staff. Also, while pupils who presented a challenge were often seen as participating more in group work, interactions with other pupils were improved in only a relatively small number of cases. Thus, the main effects of the project were centred around the staff who were directly involved and the pupils who were selected for participation because of their challenging behaviour. There is only limited evidence that the new methods of working were shared with other members of staff and that reduced levels of challenging behaviour generalised to interactions with other staff or pupils.

Staff expertise

The third area explored in the evaluation questionnaire was the development of staff expertise in the identification and recording of challenging behaviour, responding to incidents, teaching new skills and involving pupils in group activities. In most areas a high proportion of teachers indicated that they had been able to apply the relevant strategy during the project and that they were confident they could introduce similar approaches with other pupils. However, only a relatively small number reported that they had actually done so.

There are, therefore, unanswered questions regarding the extent to which expressed confidence is translated into improved practice and under what conditions this can be most effectively achieved. For example, it is quite possible that teachers correctly identified their own skills and abilities, but underestimated the extent to which practical and motivational obstacles may impede progress. While visiting the schools, project staff had provided both encouragement and an additional resource for dealing with practical difficulties. The effect of withdrawing this support is unknown and systematic evaluation was beyond the scope of this study. However, from our experience of working alongside these teachers and developing new methods of working with pupils who challenge, it seems likely that the response of the head teacher to work within the classroom, and the school in general, could have a major influence on long term outcomes.

Alternatively, it may be that teachers are not particularly accurate in identifying their own competencies; they may have exaggerated or underestimated the extent to which their skills for helping pupils with challenging behaviour had improved during the course of the project. Unfortunately, a rigorous evaluation of the impact of the in-service work on teacher competences and classroom practice, and the associated long term effects on the behaviour of pupils who present challenging behaviour, was beyond the scope and resources of this project.

Chapter 9

OVERVIEW AND IMPLICATIONS FOR PRACTICE

Educational change is technically simple and socially complex (Fullan, 1991).

This project was initiated with three broad objectives in mind:

- Collaboration with teachers and care staff to design intervention strategies for working with pupils who present problem behaviour.

- Through monitoring and evaluation, to determine interventions which can be most effectively employed in schools.

- To develop in-service training materials to disseminate the lessons learned from the study and thereby assist other teachers working with pupils who present similar challenges.

In this final chapter we briefly review the major outcomes of the study before discussing their implications for educational practice.

Prevalence and consequences of challenging behaviours

During the preliminary survey, head teachers identified 15% of pupils with severe challenging behaviours and a further 12% with problem behaviours which constituted a lesser challenge. The most frequently cited behaviours were those that resulted in physical aggression, non-compliance, distractibility for the pupil concerned or disruption in the classroom. Schools seemed to be poorly prepared to respond to the challenge presented by these behaviours. There was a notable absence of guidelines for management strategies and few school policy statements went beyond mentioning that special approaches might be required to address the needs of pupils who presented problem behaviours. Schools expected to receive very little help from agencies or professionals outside the school and there is no evidence of a co-ordinated programme of in-service training.

In the next stage of the study, teachers responsible for pupils with challenging behaviours were either interviewed (Phase I) or asked to complete a questionnaire (Phase II). This confirmed that aggression and non-compliance were among the most frequently cited reasons for identifying behaviours as problematic. Behaviours in these categories were regarded as both relatively severe but only aggression was seen as highly disruptive. Inappropriate noises were often mentioned and were rated high in respect of both severity and disruption. Socially inappropriate behaviours were rated low in respect of severity and disruption. These findings are based on very low sample sizes and clearly require further exploration. However, they do suggest that in the school context, the concept of challenging behaviour requires further elaboration and that severity and disruption are likely to be among its most salient dimensions.

Challenging behaviours have a number of adverse consequences: teachers involved in this study most frequently referred to the isolation of pupils, limited access to the curriculum, reduced opportunities for extra curricular activities and classroom disruption. Typical responses to problem behaviour were to ignore or avoid the pupil; to attempt to divert or distract and ultimately to remove him or her. None of these strategies was regarded as being particularly helpful and, not surprisingly, teachers experienced a variety of emotional responses, which were generally dealt with by talking informally to their colleagues. There was little evidence of structured support systems for staff being available within the schools or from the local authorities.

Collaboration with schools

Work with schools was based on the idea of collaboration for a number of reasons:

- First, it was important to establish methods of working which were compatible with the organisation and working practices of schools. This could only be achieved by discussion and negotiation.

- Secondly, we did not wish to be seen as experts who held privileged knowledge about pupils who challenge; instead, we wanted to share with teachers an approach to solving complex problems.

- Thirdly, we wanted to test the hypothesis that teachers already own knowledge and skills which can be deployed in working with pupils who challenge. We took the view that the introduction of technically complex procedures was neither necessary nor feasible. However, we did anticipate spending some time discussing the meaning of challenging behaviour for both the teacher and the pupil.

- Fourthly, we wanted school staff to be actively committed to the project. We hoped they would see the project as an opportunity for school and staff development. Above all, we wanted to leave schools with a sense of their own competence to address challenging behaviours and not with an increased dependence on outside agencies.

- Fifthly, we wanted to avoid giving the impression that challenging behaviour can be addressed by the application of predetermined procedures. Instead, we wanted to help schools to establish a process involving the whole school which would enable staff to respond flexibly and creatively to pupils who presented a challenge.

Collaboration was established through a series of meetings with different groups of staff and consultancy support provided by the project team. This can be briefly summarised in chronological sequence:

1. Initial contact with the head teacher and the local education authority.

2. A whole school meeting to consider:
   - the nature and scope of the project; the role of the school as a partner
   - definitions of challenging behaviour
   - the selection of pupils.

3. Collecting information on participating pupils:
   - classroom observation (shadowing) by project staff
   - observation and recording by teachers of specific behaviours
   - interview or self report questionnaire
   - Vineland Adaptive Behaviour Scales.

4. A review meeting to consider:
   - Why does the behaviour occur?
   - What can be done to reduce the occurence of challenging behaviour?
   - What can be done to encourage non-challenging behaviours?
   - Recommendations.

5. Introduce agreed strategies with consultancy support from project staff.

6. Monitoring challenging behaviours:
   - Classroom observation (shadowing) by project staff
   - Observation and recording by teachers.

7. Project evaluation:
   - Questionnaires to teachers, classroom support workers and head teachers.

8. A whole school meeting covering:

   - Feedback on the project

- In-service training; maintaining a whole school approach to pupils who challenge.

The feedback from head teachers and other staff indicated that this approach was highly successful in establishing good working relations between schools and the project team.

Strategies adopted and implemented during the project

A wide range of specific procedures were introduced during the project depending on the specific needs of individual pupils and the strengths and limitations of each school setting. When these procedures were subsequently grouped under general headings, the most frequently occurring strategies were: the introduction of a more structured day for the targeted pupils; the development of a range of educational and social activities; positive reinforcement for appropriate behaviours; establishing predictable outcomes; encouraging communication and non-verbal interactions; circulating written guidelines for other staff regarding proactive and reactive procedures. Approximately 75% of procedures which were agreed at the Review Meetings were subsequently implemented. Among the most important factors influencing implementation were the existence of effective organisational systems within the school and good staff communication within the classroom.

Did the project make a difference?

We have suggested that the efficacy of this kind of project should be measured in a number of different ways. We focused on objective measures of change applied to specific challenging behaviours together with an analysis of teachers' perceptions regarding overall satisfaction, perceived efficacy and confidence in carrying the work forward.

Classroom observation by the project staff and teacher records of challenging behaviours were limited by technical weaknesses. However, together, they provide some limited support for the view that, in the short time available, changes did occur to the extent that problem behaviours occurred less frequently or for a shorter duration. Behavioural recording is an important part of any systematic intervention strategy. In the light of the practical difficulties experienced by most teachers trying to carry out observation and recording in the classroom, we recommend that this should receive much greater attention in the future both as an integral element in staff training and as an ongoing aspect of good practice in schools.

Staff satisfaction

Most staff indicated that they were satisfied or very satisfied with the various elements of the project. However, there was very little expressed satisfaction for the support provided by head teachers. The extent to which head teachers became actively involved in supporting the project may well have had important consequences. For example, the attempt to extend the impact of the project beyond the pupils and staff directly involved seems to have been largely unsuccessful. Few teachers thought that pupils other than those selected for direct participation in the project, had benefited and there was little satisfaction in respect of positive outcomes for the school as a whole.

Perceived efficacy

Teachers believed that the strategies established with the project staff were effective in that they resulted in: changes in specific challenging behaviours; pupils being taught new skills; positive changes in teacher interactions with pupils; improved pupil interactions with classroom support workers.

Teachers' confidence in carrying the work forward

Teachers expressed confidence in their ability to record challenging behaviours although, as already noted, the extent to which systematic observation and record keeping is compatible with other classroom pressures requires further clarification. Teachers, felt able to develop and implement strategies to achieve the following outcomes: effective responses to challenging behaviours which do occur; proactive strategies to reduce the occurrence of challenging behaviours; teaching pupils with challenging behaviour new skills; involving pupils with challenging behaviour in group activities.

Teachers felt that they had been well supported by their teaching colleagues and classroom support workers during the course of the project. However, less than half the teachers responding thought the whole school strategy had been successful or moderately successful.

Discussion

The question of what needs to be done to help teachers to address the needs of pupils who present challenging behaviours is often answered in terms of developing individual professional competencies. There is ample evidence that relatively sophisticated techniques are available to address a wide range of challenging behaviours (Jones & Eayres 1993; Kiernan 1993) and it is often assumed that the solution to the management of problem behaviours in schools is for teachers to become more adept at using these techniques. In other words, to be effective, teachers must become skilled behaviour therapists. This reasoning overlooks the social and organisational complexity of schools. In this study, rather than making assumptions about what teachers needed to learn, we asked what interventions might be appropriate, given the knowledge and experience of teachers and the pressing demands of ongoing classroom activities.

Working with teachers to consider a pupil's needs and trying to understand how a particular problem behaviour 'worked' for that pupil, resulted in significant progress, given sufficient time for staff participation and a carefully structured discussion. Consideration of strategies for addressing those needs and overcoming the challenging behaviours was also productive. Most teachers were able to participate actively in the Review Meetings and either make positive suggestions or respond to proposals from others in the group. The presence of an experienced teacher on the project team acting in a consultancy role was invaluable in establishing what Fullan (1991) refers to as 'interactive professionalism' during these meetings.

In almost every case there was unanimous support for the strategies and specific procedures which were adopted. In this sense, work in school was not reliant upon technically sophisticated approaches to challenging behaviours. Instead, the emphasis was on common sense approaches which looked as if they would be workable within a particular classroom or school. It should be emphasised that while the process by which interventions were agreed was non-technical, the approaches themselves bore many similarities to interventions described in the clinical literature.

Successful implementation of agreed procedures was dependent upon a number of factors, nearly all of which concern the social and organisational context of the school. Here we refer briefly to three major influences on implementation. First, the existing organisation within the classroom and the school were crucial to the systematic introduction of new ways of working. Where teachers were poorly organised and their activities lacked a clear structure, implementation was difficult. Secondly, good working relationships between members of the classroom team and with colleagues in other parts of the school supported the introduction of new ways of working. Where good communication did not exist, changed practice was often localised and short lived. Thirdly, active support from the senior management team, especially the head teacher, was crucial during a period characterised by increased work and the uncertainty associated with developing new practice. Teachers valued both practical support, for example, the provision of cover while they attended planning meetings, and the personal commitment of senior staff to the achievement of a common goal. Unfortunately, some heads paid little more than lip service to the notion of a whole school approach and provided little or no support after the initial meetings.

The major outcome from the project is not a list of interventions which can be used in schools and matched to the needs of individual pupils. Instead, we have described a model for working in schools and the associated stages in the development of a collaborative partnership with teachers and other staff. We believe the model is practical and effective. In-service training materials designed to extend this work to other schools are available from *The British Institute of Learning Disabilities.*

As we have already noted, successful implementation of new methods of working is by no means assured. We would emphasise that the major impediments are not lack of technical competence among school staff or problems in helping teachers to learn new skills. Rather, the greatest obstacles to effective work with this group of pupils are presented by existing school practices. From this perspective, we would have to conclude that while there is an infinite number of ways in which school interventions can be undermined and eventually destroyed by existing constraints within schools, there are relatively few ways in which social and organisational factors within schools can come together to make real progress and development attainable.

Limitations of the study
To avoid confusion about what has been achieved during this project, we take this opportunity to refer briefly to the limitations inherent in the approach we have adopted, and the implications for our conclusions.

The search for causal relationships.
A traditional approach to intervention might have adopted a standard experimental design using pre - and post- intervention measures of both teaching practices and pupil outcomes. For a variety of reasons, we adopted a very different approach. Most importantly, we did not begin work in schools with any preconceived ideas about what teachers ought to be doing and we expected to learn as much from our contact with staff in schools as they would learn from us. Given this approach, we felt there was little justification for trying to describe in detail the methods used to address challenging behaviours or the level of staff knowledge about effective methods of intervention before the project was introduced into schools.

Once we had agreed with school staff on methods of working with the selected pupils, we were interested in the extent to which interventions were implemented. We also wanted to know whether there were any concomitant changes in pupil behaviours. However, when working with teachers and children within a socially complex setting, such as a school, even under ideal conditions, it is extremely difficult to tease out cause and effect relations.

While we were able to monitor the implementation of agreed methods of working with pupils, it should not be concluded that these were always new strategies or, indeed, that they would not have been introduced without support from the project staff. On the contrary, from the comments of some teachers, it seems highly probable that at least some of these procedures would have been tried anyway. Since the goal was to establish a methodology for working in collaboration with teachers and exploring strategies which they regarded as practicable, this outcome was both expected and highly desirable.

We attempted to measure changes in pupil behaviour by recording specific challenging behaviours before and after the period of intervention. In doing this we encountered a number of problems and it should be emphasised that the evidence we were able to collect is not easily interpretable. Baseline data was collected over a relatively short period of time and there was no opportunity to explore behaviour change under a return to baseline condition or to target specific behaviours for intervention while monitoring others.

Problems in behaviour recording

The approach to recording during the project was a product both of necessity and design. Our intention was to explore how much schools could do for themselves, not how much we could do for them. We sought to increase their autonomy, not their dependence on other professionals. For this reason, we invited teachers to participate in recording target behaviours. However, without a reliable backup resource for data collection, it was impossible to monitor teacher recording methods effectively or to collect comparison data to establish inter-rater reliability. Consequently, behaviour recording was uneven in terms of quantity and of a largely unknown quality.

The project officer undertook classroom observations both before and after the interventions had been introduced. These were planned as part of the process of collaboration to ensure that she was fully familiar with the pupils involved in the study and the social and educational context within which problem behaviours occurred. She had insufficient time to carry out additional behaviour recording and it would have required a significant time commitment to arrange with teachers for joint observation sessions, to provide additional data for measures of inter-rater reliability.

Involving teachers in making records of challenging behaviours was a valuable exercise which underlined social and organisational difficulties associated with the introduction of relatively simple data collection procedures in schools. Judged from the responses to the evaluation questionnaires, the introduction of an in-service training session to prepare staff for the task was moderately successful. This session, together with increased support from the project staff during Phase II, resulted in a high completion rate for pre - and post - recording. However, there is little doubt that observation and recording of behaviours is an activity which these teachers found irksome and of little practical relevance. The integration of methods of behaviour recording with good educational practice is a subject which requires further attention.

The time frame

The project was funded for a period of eighteen months in total. Given the desirability of working within more than five schools, the research design allowed for a maximum time commitment of two school terms in each phase of the study. In any school-based intervention study, evidence of change is likely to be positively correlated with the duration of the project; there is no optimal time interval for intervention or indeed any limit to the amount of time which might usefully be committed to such a project. Conversely, there is no prior justification for establishing a minimum period of intervention as a critical variable. However, the experience of the project staff involved in this study was that the limited time available significantly reduced opportunities for establishing good practice which could eventually become self sustaining. It also required the maintenance of a delicate balance between consultancy support, to promote the development of good practice, and time devoted to monitoring and evaluation.

The ingredients of successful school based intervention

We have described the development of a Whole School Approach to working with pupils who present a challenge as a process which begins with the identification of 'problem behaviours' and culminates in the implementation and evaluation of intervention strategies. While working in nine schools, we met with varying degrees of success in establishing this process. During the research we were not able to address directly the question of why schools responded to the project in different ways, but our experience of working in classrooms alongside teachers enabled us to generate a number of specific hypotheses. In this section we present these hypotheses in the form of a model (Figure 9:2).

This model presents the key components of a process approach and describes the resources which will determine how successfully a school is able to respond to pupils who present a challenge. All challenging behaviour at school occurs in a rich social context which determines how the behaviour is interpreted and evaluated and, secondly, what action will be taken. Resources are those features of the social and educational context which have implications for the process by which schools identify and respond to 'problem behaviours'. Schools which are well resourced will be better able to respond to inappropriate behaviour and will be less likely to seek external support than those which have few resources. Furthermore, well resourced schools are more likely to respond to challenging behaviours in ways which minimise the adverse consequences for the pupil concerned, his or her peers and members of staff.

A precise specification of the resources which are available to support a Whole School Approach would have a number of advantages. First, it would enable schools to conduct an audit of their own resources and thus determine whether they could successfully introduce a Whole School Approach. Secondly, it would help to identify areas which might be targeted in a school development plan. Thirdly, for schools which are experiencing difficulty in working with pupils who present a challenge, it would provide a framework for identifying relative strengths and weaknesses.

School-based resources for responding to challenging behaviours

There are three kinds of resources which can be described and measured. The classification proposed here corresponds to the analysis presented in Chapter 6 which described intervention strategies according to whether they focused upon individual teacher-pupil interactions; classroom management and curriculum planning; or approaches with implications for the school as a whole. While the resource categories described here are based upon the experiences of the project team, it should be emphasised that the examples are illustrative and, to our knowledge, have not been tested empirically.

Personal resources refer to the characteristics and qualities of individual members of staff. They include personality traits; styles of interaction with pupils and colleagues; attitudes towards unconventional behaviour; views on child development and the role of education; confidence and assertiveness.

Personal resources are likely to affect the extent to which bizarre or inappropriate behaviours are tolerated and how they are interpreted. They will also influence the way in which individual members of staff typically interact with pupils when they display challenging behaviours. The following is a provisional list of the factors which are likely to affect the way in which adults interpret behaviours and interact with pupils who they perceive as challenging .

Personal resources for responding to challenging behaviours

Personality factors: introversion; extroversion; anxiety; susceptibility to stress.

Attitudes to unconventional behaviour and lifestyles; education; child development.

Values regarding people with learning disabilities

Social skills and established styles of interaction; confidence and assertiveness.

Self-image; stability of personal relationships.

Gender.

Technical resources refer to the broader range of professional skills and competencies required for working effectively with pupils with severe learning disabilities. They include the knowledge and skills directly relevant to the management of pupils who challenge, for example, an understanding of the theory and practice of behaviour modification or gentle teaching, as well as specific techniques which have been developed in order to respond to particular pupils. Methods of recording behaviour and experience in using published assessment tools would also be included. The following is a provisional list of technical resources which are likely to influence

(a) any systematic attempt to monitor and eradicate challenging behaviour

(b) the development, implementation and maintenance of planned intervention strategies.

Technical resources for responding to challenging behaviour

Skills for observing and recording behaviours.

Skills in classroom organisation and management

Skills in curriculum design and delivery

Knowledge of specific approaches, for example, behaviour modification or Gentle Teaching

Specific management techniques developed for working with individual pupils

Organisational resources are concerned with those features which characterise the school as a physical and social unit. They embrace buildings and equipment (for example, a large soft play area which is usually available for pupils who are not coping in a classroom), administrative and managerial systems to co-ordinate and monitor the work of individual members of staff and the existence of policies and procedures designed to support staff working with pupils who challenge.

Organisational resources for responding to challenging behaviour

Buildings, internal and external space, equipment and facilities.

Management systems for recording and sharing information, monitoring performance, developing teamwork.

Availability of support for staff: creative (i.e. suggestions about what to do); practical (hands on help); and personal (monitoring and replenishing personal resources).

Policies on working with pupils who challenge.

Opportunities for staff training (developing technical resources).

Resources are inter-related

There is a strong likelihood that changes in the availability of one type of resource will have an indirect effect on other resources. For example, a head teacher who monitors staff performance and provides support for teachers working with pupils who challenge is likely to increase the ability of staff to withstand some of the stresses which arise from working with aggressive or violent pupils. Similarly, training in procedures for managing violence and aggression is likely to increase staff confidence. On the other hand, excellent resources in one area (for example, personal resources) are unlikely to be used to their full potential if they are not supported with at least adequate resources in other areas. Indeed, it is likely that extremely poor resources in one area might lead to excessive demands on other resources to the point where they disintegrate altogether. An example of this would be inexperienced staff with access to few technical resources being asked to work with extremely challenging pupils without appropriate organisational support. In such circumstances, even very abundant personal resources are, sooner or later, likely to be overwhelmed. The relationship between different resources which may be deployed in responding to people who challenge is shown in Fig. 9.1.

Figure 9.1

Inter-relationships among resources for responding to challenging behaviours

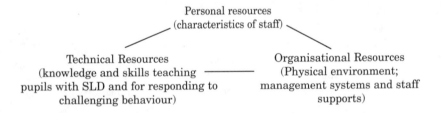

The impact of school-based resources on a Whole School Approach

There are three points at which the existence of these resources will influence the way in which staff respond to pupils who challenge.

1. The identification of challenging behaviours

The model suggests that before responding to pupil behaviours teachers make intuitive judgments about whether they are positive, neutral/acceptable or 'challenging'. The category 'neutral or acceptable' includes all behaviours which are not explicitly evaluated as being 'positive' or 'negative'. This is not to say that neutral behaviours lack developmental or educational significance; only that they are not registered by teachers as worthy of a specific response. Positive behaviours are those which are recognised as being particularly salient in terms of the teacher's expectations for that pupil in the context of ongoing classroom activities. Positive behaviours are likely to evoke some form of encouragement or reward. Challenging behaviours are those which the teacher recognises as being problematic for the pupil concerned, for other pupils in the group or for members of staff. The 'definition' or interpretative statements which have been put forward to assist in the identification of challenging behaviours (see Chapter 2) entail a behavioural continuum ranging from 'positive' (or appropriate) through neutral to 'negative' or challenging behaviours. The position of any specific behaviour on the continuum will depend upon a number of factors including the topography of the behaviour (the precise actions which are performed) and the social setting in which the behaviour occurs.

CHALLENGING	NEUTRAL	POSITIVE
Throwing objects in the classroom	Throwing objects in the playground	Throwing objects at a target in a hand-eye co-ordination task

While staff responses to positive behaviours are important in their own right, the model is only elaborated with respect to behaviours which are identified as 'challenging'.

From this it is clear that the definitions of challenging behaviour provided by Emerson et al (1987)and Zarkowska and Clements (1988 depend upon teachers making a social, and therefore subjective, judgment about the likely impact or consequences of specific behaviours. For example, to use the definition provided by Emerson et al, the teacher is required to make a judgment about the likely consequences for the pupil concerned, his/her peers and other adults who work with him or her in the short term (risk of injury) and over a much longer period (future access to ordinary community facilities).

This suggests that the categorisation of behaviours by staff cannot be derived from the application of a rule or algorithm; instead, it is based on the relationship between the behaviour which the pupils displays and the personal resources which the member of staff brings to the classroom. First, it is proposed that the personal resources of staff will determine the social, developmental and educational significance they attribute to specific behaviours and therefore the likelihood of those behaviours being seen as problematic. For example, it seems likely that staff will vary in the value they place on social conformity when working with pupils who present bizarre or severely inappropriate behaviours. Whereas some staff may ignore (or categorise as 'neutral') behaviours which are socially inappropriate, but have little impact on the pupil's educational and developmental progress, others may be more concerned about potentially stigmatising behaviours, irrespective of their potential role in development and/or education.

Secondly, it is proposed that personal resources will influence the sensitivity or tolerance of staff to bizarre or disruptive behaviours. Some staff are likely to have a relatively high tolerance for disruptive or socially inappropriate behaviour while others will have a much lower tolerance and this will affect the probability that specific behaviours are categorised as challenging. It also seems likely that staff tolerance will interact with other pupil characteristics. For example, a male member of staff may find it easier to tolerate inappropriate sexual behaviour presented by a male pupil compared to similar behaviour presented by a female pupil.

Technical resources concerned with the teacher's ability to work with pupils with severe learning disabilities are also likely to influence the initial state of identification. On the one hand, pupils are more likely to present disorganised and disruptive behaviours in poorly organised classrooms. On the other hand, it may be the case that problematic behaviours are more visible in classrooms with a high degree of structure and where staff establish clear expectations about pupil behaviours.

The extent to which behaviours are identified as posing a challenge is likely to have far reaching consequences for pupils and staff in schools. First, the failure to identify a behaviour as presenting a 'challenge' may delay formal assessment, staff discussion and a planned programme to respond to the behaviour. On the other hand, a behaviour may not be recognised as challenging because the personal and technical resources of the staff enable them to work successfully with the pupil in spite of the fact that he or she presents some potentially problematic behaviours. Among the pupils in this study, Harry was identified as displaying serious non-compliant behaviour, not by the staff who worked with him on a daily basis, but by those who came into contact with him intermittently. Observation indicated that while Harry presented very similar behaviours across settings, his regular teacher and her support worker had evolved a very simple 'no nonsense' approach involving clear expectations, consistency and firmness. Their personal resources enabled them to work successfully with Harry so that they were ambivalent about identifying 'non-compliance' as 'challenging'. Where staff are able to draw on few personal and technical resources, it seems likely that they will categorise a disproportionate number of pupils as 'challenging'.

Further research is required to clarify the range of personal and technical resources which impact upon the identification of challenging behaviours. This would establish whether or not it is possible to construct a measure which incorporates the concept of 'challenge' as a relationship between specific behaviours and the context in which they occur. In the absence of such a measure, studies of prevalence must either focus on topographic descriptions of behaviour or rely upon staff perceptions of the meaning of 'challenging' and the inherent unreliability of such an approach.

Identification of Challenging Behaviour ⟵ Personal Resources
⟵ Technical Resources

2. Assessment

In this project, we have described assessment as the process by which information on a pupil's challenging behaviour is collected and evaluated. Once the behaviour has been clearly described, the key questions are:

- How frequently does it occur and with what severity and/or duration?

- What are the consequences for the pupil and those around him/her? Why does the behaviour occur?

- What action may be taken to reduce the behaviour or diminish the consequences of the behaviour?

Collecting evidence to answer these questions requires the application of technical resources. By technical we do not mean complex or sophisticated clinical techniques. Instead, we use the term 'technical' to refer to a planned and systematically applied set of procedures which focus on the pupil and the behaviour which has been identified as problematic. The ability to organise and implement such a systematic assessment varies from teacher to teacher and from school to school. On the basis of the findings from this study, it is doubtful that many schools possess the necessary technical resources. Most schools would require highly specific in-service training and, probably, continuing access to support from outside agencies such as a schools psychological service or a clinical psychologist with experience of working with people with challenging behaviour.

Assessment of Challenging Behaviours
and Recommendations for Intervention ⟵—————— Technical Resources

3. Action

We have described action to address challenging behaviours as being targeted at the pupil, the classroom or the school as a whole. The analysis of the factors which had a positive or negative impact on the implementation of intervention strategies suggests the range of resources associated with successful outcomes. At the level of staff competence in working with pupils with severe learning disabilities, technical resources will determine whether interventions are introduced into a relatively well planned and organised teaching environment in which activities are designed to match the strengths and needs of individual pupils. Technical resources specifically concerned with knowledge and skills relating to pupils who challenge will also influence the way in which some recommendations are translated into classroom practice. However, many strategies employed in this study did not require staff to exercise any special skill or expertise. In many ways personal resources such as enthusiasm, determination and the flexibility to adapt teaching practice to accommodate an intervention procedure seemed to have had a much greater influence on implementation.

Finally, and perhaps most importantly, school resources are likely to make a major contribution to the successful implementation of intervention strategies. Space and physical resources are likely to determine not only what strategies are feasible, but how easily they can be introduced. The existence of established management systems with effective methods of communication between staff, and a head teacher with good management skills, are prerequisites to the successful introduction of a Whole School Approach (see, for example, Fullan, 1991). In schools where the head teacher is in close touch with classroom practice and understands the relative strengths and needs of different members of staff, he or she is in a better position to provide continuous support and encouragement while intervention strategies were being implemented.

Action on Challenging Behaviours ⟶ Personal Resources
⟵ Technical Resources
⟶ Organisational Resources

In addition to providing a summary which can help schools evaluate how far they possess the range of resources needed to respond to pupils who challenge, this model sets out an agenda for further research. The resources identified here are based on informal observation during a school based study and the analysis of the relationship between the process of responding to challenging behaviours and the availability of such resources is purely speculative. However, until we have a better understanding of what resources really make a difference and how to determine whether or not specific resources are available in schools, pupils who display violent, disruptive or inappropriate behaviour will continue to pose a challenge in schools.

The model which has been briefly outlined here has a number of advantages. First, it describes the richness and complexity of one social setting within which challenging behaviours occur. Secondly, it emphasises how little is currently known about the interaction between the behaviour of pupils with severe learning difficulties and various aspects of the school environment. To date, very little work has addressed the factors which influence staff responses to challenging behaviours and the capacity of schools to introduce and maintain planned interventions. While this gap in our knowledge remains, it is difficult to determine how schools compare regarding their management of pupils who present a challenge and, also, what can most usefully be done to help schools respond more effectively. This leads to the third potential benefit from such a model in that it sets out an agenda for further research to establish those resources which have the greatest impact on a school's capacity to respond to pupils who challenge. This, in turn, would make it possible to evaluate the strengths and weaknesses of individual schools according to their available resources. Additional resources could then be selectively targeted to compensate for specific areas of weakness and to build upon resource strengths. For example, one school might need help in developing a policy on challenging behaviour, while another might benefit most from intensive in-service training to help staff to improve their procedures of observation and recording.

Figure 9.2
Resources to Support a Whole School Approach to Pupils with Challenging Behaviour

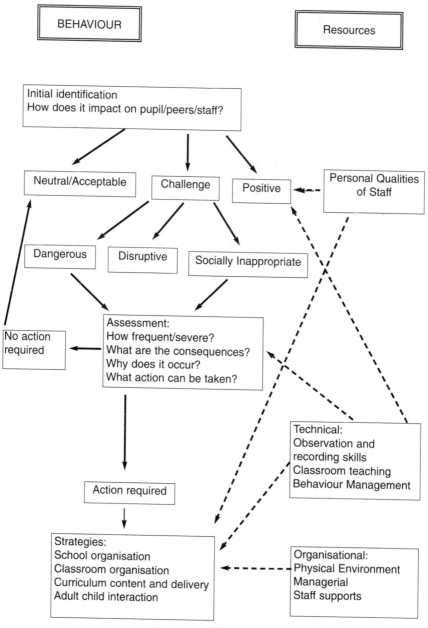

Conclusion

In this book, we have described one small-scale project concerned with pupils with severe learning difficulties who present challenging behaviours. During the project, we worked closely with teachers and other staff in schools to establish practical strategies which can reduce the level of challenging behaviours and help pupils to participate in educational and recreational activities.

While acknowledging that clinical research has generated a number of treatment approaches with proven effectiveness, we were also acutely aware that the technical sophistication of many of these approaches meant that they would not be easily established in schools. Rather than focusing on the introduction of new technical procedures, we sought to establish a process which would engage staff in a variety of relevant activities. These included selecting pupils for participation in the study; identification of specific behaviours; observation and record keeping; thinking about the behaviour from the pupil's perspective; planning new ways of working with pupils; implementing agreed procedures. Involvement of staff in these activities achieved two objectives: first, it provided a working example of a strategy for responding to challenging behaviour and, secondly, it provided opportunities for staff to review and reformulate the way in which they thought about, and worked with, pupils with challenging behaviours. We hoped that direct engagement in this process would provide staff with new says of conceptualising challenging behaviours and a structure which they could use to develop individualised strategies for working with other pupils who presented a challenge.

The approach was largely successful. The staff in each school selected pupils who could be involved in the project and the classroom staff responsible for each pupil identified specific challenging behaviours. With the help of the project team, more detailed information was collected and presented at the review meetings. At the end of the review meetings, a number of specific recommendations for intervention were agreed. Between 75% and 80% of the recommendations were implemented by classroom teachers and their assistants. Most staff also participated in collecting observational data although the consistency with which records were made could have been improved. At the end of the project, most staff reported that they had benefited by being engaged in this process and that they felt confident in their ability to employ a similar approach when working with other pupils.

In addition to the opportunities afforded to individual members of staff and to schools for learning about ways of working with pupils who challenge, there are a number of other specific outcomes which are likely to be of interest to teachers, other professionals with responsibility for pupils who present challenging behaviours, educational researchers, and those responsible for educational policy for pupils with severe learning difficulties.

First, the project demonstrated the success of a process approach to school change. It is suggested that the main features of this approach, described in Chapters 5, 6 and 7, could be used to help staff in other schools to develop effective strategies for working with pupils who challenge.

Secondly, while it is important to design intervention strategies in relation to the strengths and needs of each pupil, the analysis of the Review Meeting recommendations in Chapter 6 indicated that a relatively small number of strategies were repeated with different pupils. These ten positive approaches provide a short list of practical strategies. None of the ten approaches involve risks for the pupil and all are designed to be implemented in classroom settings. All ten approaches could be introduced by qualified teachers without additional training or specialist knowledge. (A practical guide and commentary on these approaches can be found in Harris, 1995).

Thirdly, the workshop materials used to provide the feedback and project overview to the participating schools have been further developed and field tested in other schools. They introduce the process approach employed in the project using a series of practical activities and exercises presented in five sessions over a period of two days or an equivalent period of time.

Finally, during the project it was possible to comment upon some of the factors which contributed to successful outcomes in different schools. In this chapter, these preliminary observations have been elaborated into a more detailed model of the process by which schools identify, assess and respond to challenging behaviours. It is suggested that each stage of the process will be influenced by the availability of personal, technical and organisational resources. Schools which have adequate resources will have a high tolerance for unusual or socially inappropriate behaviours; they will be able to prepare detailed assessments of specific behaviours; and design and implement a range of appropriate strategies. In contrast, schools with few resources, or resources which are inadequate in relation to the challenge presented by pupil behaviours, will have a low tolerance of typical behaviours; they will find it difficult to carry out detailed assessments; and they will struggle to develop and implement appropriate procedures. The model presented sets out a fresh agenda for research on challenging behaviour among pupils with severe learning difficulties and a framework for developing improved school-based intervention.

References

Blunden, R. and Allen, D. 1987
Facing the Challenge: An Ordinary Life for People with Learning Difficulties and Challenging Behaviour.
London: King's Fund Centre.

Dyer, K., Dunlap, and Winterling, V. 1990
Effects of choice making on the serious problem behaviours of students with severe handicaps
Journal of Applied Behaviour Analysis, 23, 4, 5 1 5-524.

Campbell, D.T. and Stanley, J.C. 1966
Experimental and Quasi-Experimental Designs.
Chicago: Rand and McNally.

Carr, E.G. and Durand, V.M. 1985
Reducing behaviour problems through functional communication training.
Journal of Applied Behaviour Analysis. 18, 2, 111-126.

Carr, E.G., Taylor, J.C. and Robinson, S. 1991
The effects of severe behaviour problems in children on the teaching behaviour of adults.
Journal of Applied Behaviour Analysis, 24, 3, 523-535.

Cornick, M. and Cornick,T. 1994
Quality management and training for staff working with people with severe learning difficulty and challenging behaviour using a transdisciplinary model. In J. Harris and J.Corbett (eds) *Training and Professional Development: An Interdisciplinary Perspective for those working with People who have Severe Learning Disabilities. BILD Seminar Papers No.5.*
Kidderminster: British Institute of Learning Disabilities.

Cowdery, G.E., Iwata, B.A.and Pace, G.M. 1990
Effects and side effects of DRO as a treatment for self-injurious behaviour. *Journal of Applied Behaviour Analysis.* 23, 4, 497-506.

Cuskelly, M. and Dadds, M. 1992
Behavioural problems in children with Down's Syndrome and their siblings.
Journal of Child Psychology and Psychiatry. 23, 4, 749-761.

Department for Education 1994
Pupil Behaviourand Discipline.
London: DFE Publication Centre.

Department of Educationand Science and The Welsh Office. 1989
Discipline in Schools. Report of the Committee of Enquiry chaired by Lord Elton.
London: HMSO.

Donnellan, A.M., Mirenda, P.L., Mesaros, R.A. and Fassbender, L.L.
Analysing the communication functions of aberrant behaviour.
Journal of Association for Persons with Severe Handicaps 3, 201-212.

Donnellan, A.M., LaVigna G., Negri-Shoultz, N. and Fassbender, L.L. 1988
Progress without Punishment: Effective Approaches for Learners with behaviour Problems.
New York: Teachers College Press.

Durand, V.M. 1990
Severe Behaviour Problems: A Functional Communication Trainina Approach. New York: Guilford Press.

Durand, V.M. and Kishi, G. 1987
Reducing severe behaviour problems among persons with dual sensory impairments: an evaluation of a technical assistance model. *Journal of the Association of Persons with Severe Handicaps.* 12, 1, 2-10.

Dyer, K. and Dunlap, G. 1990
The effects of choice making on the serious problem behaviours of students with severe handicaps. *Journal of Applied Behaviour Analysis,* 23, 4,515-524.

Emerson, E. 1992

Self-injurious behaviour: An overview of recent trends in epidemiological and behavioural research. *Mental Handicap Research*, 5, 1 .

Emerson, E., Barrett, S., Bell, C., Cummings, R.,Hughes, H., McCool, C., Toogood, A. and Mansell, J. 1987

The Special Development Team: Developing Services for People with Severe Learning Difficulties and Challenging Behaviours. University of Kent, Institute of Social and Applied Psychology.

Emerson, E., Cambridge, P. and Harris, P. 1991

Evaluating the Challenge London: King's Fund Centre.

Foxen, T.and McBrien, J. 1981

The EDY course for mental handicap practitioners Manchester: Manchester University Press.

Foxx, R.M. 1990

Harry": A ten year follow-up of the successful treatment of a self-injurious man. *Research in Developmental Disabilities.* 11, 67-76.

Fullan, M.G. 1991

The New Meaning of Educational Change. London: Cassell.

Gaboney, P. 1991

Self-injurious behaviour: A unitary phenomenon or a set of diverse behaviours? *British Journal of Special Education.* 18, 2, 59-63.

Gath, A. and Gumley, D. 1986

Behaviour problems in retarded children with special reference to Down's Syndrome. *British Journal of Psychiatry.* 1 49,1 56-1 61

Griffin, J.C., Ricketts, R.W., Williams, D.E., Locke, B.Altmeyer, B.K. and Starke, M.T. 1987

A community survey of self-injurious behaviour among developmentally disabled children and adolescents. *Hospital and Community Psychiatry.* 38, 9, 959-963.

Harris, J. 1993

Innovations in Educating Children with Severe Learning Difficulties. Chorley, Lancs: Lisieux Hall.

Harris, J. and Cook, M. 1995

A Whole School Approach to Working with Pupils with Severe Learning Difficulties and Challenging Behaviour. First Draft Publications. Kidderminster: British Institute of Learning Disabilities.

Harris, J. 1995

Responding to Pupils with Severe Learning Disabilities who present Challenging Behaviours. *British Journal of Special Education.* Accepted for publication September 1995.

Holmes, N., Shah, A. and Wing, L. 1982

The Disability assessment Schedule: A brief screening device for use with the mentally retarded. *Psychological Medicine.* 12, 879-890.

Horner, R.H., Dunlap, G. Koegel, R.L., Carr, E.G., Sailor, W., Anderson, J.,Albin, R.W.and O'Neill, R. E. 1990.

Toward a technology of 'non-aversive' behavioural support. *Journal of the Association of Persons with Severe Handicaps,* 15, 3, 125 132.

Iwata, B.A., Pace, G.M. Kalsher, M.J., Cowdery, G. and Cataldo, M.F. 1990

Experimental analysis and extinction of self-injurious escape behaviour. Iournal of Applied Behaviour Analysis, 23,1, 23-27.

Janney, R.E. and Meyer, L.H. 1990

A consultation model to support integrated educational services for students with severe disabilities and challenging behaviours. *Journal of the Association of Persons with Severe Handicaps.* 15, 3, 186-199.

Jones, R.S.P. and Eayrs, C.B. (eds) 1993

Challenging Behaviour and Intellectual Disability: A Psychological Perspective. Clevedon: BILD Publications.

Kidd, C.B. and Innes, G. (1964)

The prevalence of mental subnormality in two regions. Some comparisons between north east Scotland and Northern Ireland. *Ulster Medical Journal.* 36, 139-144.

Kiernan, C. (ed) (1994)

Research to Practice: Implications of Research on the Challenging Behaviour of People with Learning Disabilities. Clevedon: BILD Publications.

Kiernan, C. and Kiernan, D. (1994)

Challenging behaviour in schools for pupils with severe learning difficulties. *Mental Handicap Research.* 7, 3, 177-201.

Kiernan, C. and Bliss, V.

Preparing professionals to work with people who have learning disabilities and challenging behaviour. In J. Harris and J.Corbett (eds) *Training and Professional Development: An Interdisciplinary Perspective for those working with People who have Severe Learning Disabilities. BILD Seminar Papers No.5.* Kidderminster: British Institute of Learning Disabilities.

Kushlik, A. and Cox, G. 1968

The ascertained prevalence of mental subnormality in the Wessex region on July 1 1963. *In Proceedings of the 1st Congress of the Association for the Scientific Study of Mental Deficiency* (Ed. B. W. Richards). p661-663. Reigate: Michael Jackson.

Lovett, H. 1985

Cognitive Counselling and Persons with Special Needs: Adapting Behavioural Approaches to the Social Context. New York: Praeger.

Luiselli, J.K. 1990

Recent developments in non-aversive treatment: a review of rationale, methods and recommendations. In A.C. Repp and N.N. Singh (eds) *Perspectives on the Use of Non-aversive and Aversive Interventions for Persons with Developmental Disabilities.* Sycamore, Ill: Sycamore Publishing.

McDonnell, A., Deardon, R. and Richens, A. 1991

Management of violence and aggression: Part One - Setting up a Training System. *Mental Handicap.* 19, 2, 77-82.

McGaughey, R.E.and Jones, R.S.P. 1992

The effectiveness of Gentle Teaching. *Mental Handicap,* 20,1, 7-14.

McGee, J.J., Menolascino, F.J., Hobbs, D.C.and Menousek, P.E. 1987

Gentle Teaching: A Non-aversive Approach to helping Persons with Mental Retardation. New York: Human Sciences Press.

Meyer, L. and Janney, R. 1989

User-friendly measures of meaningful outcomes: evaluating behavioural interventions. *Journal of the Association of Persons with Severe Handicaps.* 14, 4, 263-270.

Mittler, P. 1993

Teacher Education for Special Educational Needs. Policy Options for Special Education needs (3). Stafford: National Association of Special Educational Needs

Murphy, G. and Oliver, C. 1987   Decreasing undesirable behaviour. In W. Yule and J. Carr (eds) Behaviour Modification for People with MentaL Handicaps (2nd). London: Croom Helm.

O'Brien, S. and Repp, A.C. 1990   Reinforcement-based reductive procedures: a review of 20 years of their use with persons with severe or profound retardation. *Journal of the Association for Persons with Severe Handicaps,* 15, 3, 148-159.

Oliver, C., Murphy, G. and Corbett, J.A. 1987   Self-injurious behaviour in people with mental handicaps: a total population study. *Journal of Mental Deficiency Research.* 31, 147-162.

Putnam, N. and Stein, M. 1985   Self-inflicted injuries in childhood. Clinical Pediatrics, 24, 9, 514-517.

Quine, L. 1986   Behaviour problems in severely mentally handicapped children. *Psychological Medicine.* 16, 895-907.

Qureshi, H. and Alborz, A. 1992   Epidemiology of challenging behaviour. *Mental Handicap Research.* 5. 2.130-145.

Quay, H. C. and Peterson, D.R. 1983   *Interim Manual for the Revised Behaviour Probem Checklist.* (1st Edition). (no other details) .

Repp, A.C., Felce, D. and Barton, L.E. 1988   Basing the treatment of stereotypic and self-injurious behaviours on hypotheses of their causes. *Journal of Applied Behaviour Analysis,* 21, 281-289.

Sparrow, S. S., Balla, D.A. and Cicchetti, D. V. 1984   *Vineland Adaptive Behaviour Scales. Interview Edition.* Survey Form Manual. Minnesota: American Guidance Service.

Tarnowski, K., Mulick, J.A. and Rasnake, L.K. 1990   Acceptability of behavioural interventions for self injurious behaviour: replication and interinstitutional comparisons. *American Journal of Mental Retardation.* 95, 2,182-187.

Tobin, D. 1994   The inspection of special schools for pupils with severe learning difficulties. *The SLD Experience.* No.10,1-4.

Wacker, D.P., Steege, M.W., Northup, J. Sasso, G., Berg, W., Reimers, T., Cooper, L., Cigrand, K. and Donn, L. 1990   A component analysis of functional communication training across three topographies of severe behaviour problems. *Journal of Applied Behaviour Analysis.* 23, 417-429.

Wing, L. 1971   Severely retarded children in a London area: prevalence and provision of services. *Psychological Medicine,* 1, 405-415.

Winchel, R. and Stanley, M. 1991   Self-injurious behaviour: A review of the behaviour and biology of self-mutilation. *American Journal of Psychiatry.* 148, 3, 306-317.

Wolf, M.M. 1978   Social Validity: The case for subjective measurement in how applied behaviour analysis is finding its heart. *Journal of Applied Behaviour Analysis.* 11, 203-214.

Zarkowska, E. and Clements, J. 1988   Problem Behaviour and People with Severe Learning Disabilities: A Practical Guide to a Constructional Approach. London: Croom Helm.

APPENDIX ONE

CONTENTS

Letter to head teachers

Schools survey questionnaire (Chapter 4)

Semi-structured interview for staff (Chapter 5)

Behaviour recording sheets for staff (Chapter 7)

Evaluation questionnaires for staff (Chapter 8)

Evaluation questionnaires for head teachers (Chapter 8)

Evaluation questionnaires for classroom support workers (Chapter 8)

SCHOOLS SURVEY - LETTER TO HEAD TEACHERS
(Chapter 4)

Dear

Your Special Needs Advisor,   , may have spoken to you
recently about a project, run by the British Institute of Learning Disabilities and the
University of Birmingham, which aims to develop school-based services for children
with severe learning difficulties and challenging behaviour. It would be of considerable
help to us in initiating the project if you could provide us with information by answer-
ing the attached questionnaire.

We are aware that topics such as challenging behaviour and severe learning difficulties
raise numerous issues regarding definitions, and investigation of the varied perceptions of challenging behaviour will form part of the project. However, for the purposes
of this initial collection of information, the children under consideration are those
whose behaviour, within the context of your school, :-

prevents their participation in appropriate educational activities; often isolates them
from their peers; may affect the learning and functioning of other pupils; drastically
reduces their opportunities for involvement in ordinary community activities; makes
excessive demands on teachers, staff, and resources; may place the child or others in
physical danger; and makes the possibilities for future placement difficult.

We realise that completion of a questionnaire such as this can be time-consuming, but
we feel that the information gathered will be of considerable use in providing the background knowledge from which we can work to develop school-based services for this
group of children, and also in selection of the most appropriate schools for "in-depth"
study. All the information received will, of course, be treated with the utmost confidentiality. We hope that you will feel able to help us in this important and necessary
project.

If you would like further information, please do not hesitate to contact the project officer,
Margaret Cook, on 0121-414-4832 (direct line).

Thank you for your co-operation. We look forward to your early reply.

Yours sincerely,

Margaret Cook   John Harris
(Project Officer)   (Director, BILD)

SCHOOLS SURVEY QUESTIONNAIRE (Chapter 4)

1. BUILDINGS AND SERVICES:-

a) How many pupils do you have on register?

b) What age group(s) do you cover? (please tick)

Nursery................   Reception................   Infant................   Junior................

Middle (9-13)................   Secondary................   16-19................

c) How many teaching staff do you have?

Full-time................   Part-time................

d) How many classroom based non-teaching staff? (e.g. classroom support assistants)

Full-time................   Part-time................

e) How many supervisory staff at lunch and break-times?................

f) As a head-teacher do you have regular teaching duties?

Yes (full-time)................   No................

Yes, part-time (please indicate approx. percentage of week)................

g) How many a) classrooms and b) additional teaching spaces do you have that are regularly used for teaching?

a)................   b)................

h) Briefly describe any special facilities e.g. hydrotherapy pool, outdoor play space, special unit.

i) Please add any other information regarding school buildings and facilities:

....

....

....

j) Do you have involvement with other agencies and services? Please tick and indicate frequency of visits:

	Daily	Weekly	H/term	Termly	Less
L.E.A. support services (e.g. Advisor, advisory teachers)					
Educational psychologist					
Clinical psychologist					
Physiotherapy					
Speech therapy					
Schools' medical officer					
Social services					
Other (please indicate)					

k) Please add any other relevant information regarding services:-

....

....

....

....

....

2. SCHOOL POLICY:

a) Does the school have a written operate policy dealing with its aims and objectives, covering for example, such issues as the extent of integration, liaison with parents, and management of difficult behaviour?

If Yes, a copy would be appreciated.
If no, please briefly outline your broad aims below:

b) Who was involved in development of this policy? (e.g. staff, parents, governors, L.E.A. advisors, psychologist)

3. YOUR PERSPECTIVE:

If your school was selected for in-depth involvement in the project, how do you feel that the project could help you?

4. PUPILS WITH CHALLENGING BEHAVIOUR:

a) How many pupils do you have whom you regard as presenting a severe problem for you and your staff? (please refer to description in covering letter).

b) What are the ages of the pupils identified? (please indicate numbers in each year group):

Nursery............ Reception .... Infant .... Junior ....

Secondary: 11-13 .... 13-16 .... Post 16 ....

c) How would you describe the severe problems presented by these pupils?

d) How many other pupils would you describe as presenting challenging behaviours?

e) What are the ages of the pupils identified in d)?

Nursery/Reception............ Infant............ Junior............

Secondary: 11-13 .... 13-16 .... Post 16 ....

F) How would you describe the behaviour problems presented by these pupils?

5. GENERAL APPROACHES TO CHALLENGING BEHAVIOUR:

a) Do you have a general approach to the management of challenging behaviour, e.g. a behaviourist approach, use of Gentle Teaching? Please outline below:-

b) Do you have guidelines/accepted strategies for responding to crisis situations? Please outline below:-

c) Have you made any arrangements for the preparation of staff for dealing with challenging behaviour? Please outline below:-

d) Do you receive any help from other agencies, e.g. L.E.A. support services, or educational psychologist in the management of your pupils who present challenging behaviour? Please outline below:-

Thank you for your help and co-operation in completing this questionnaire. Information about the progress of the project will be disseminated as it becomes available.

SEMI-STRUCTURED INTERVIEW FOR STAFF

1. The child and his / her behaviour

1. What does this child do that creates problems for staff? Can you describe the behaviour that creates the problems?

Prompt: If more than one behaviour which creates problems, repeat questions 2 to 7 for each behaviour.

2. Would you describe this behaviour as a severe problem? If yes, why do you think that it is a severe problem?
Frequency (hourly, daily, more than once a day, weekly, etc.) Intensity (on a scale 1 to 5)?

3. In what ways does the child's behaviour create problems for him/herself?

4. How does the child's behaviour create problems for other children?

5. How often does this behaviour occur? Hourly? More than once every hour? At least once a day? Weekly? Less than once a week?

6. Is there any pattern to the behaviour? For example, does it tend to occur in certain situations or at certain times of the day or in certain places?

7. Are you able to predict when a problem is going to arise? What do you look for?

8. As far as you know is the child receiving drugs/medication at the present time? If so:

a) What are the drugs for?

b) Do you feel that they are helpful?

c) How frequently are they taken?

d) Are you aware of any side effects?

2. Staff responses to challenging behaviour

1. What do you do when child behaves in the way you have described? Do you:
a) ignore or try to avoid the problem in some way; b) attempt to divert the child or distract him/her with other activities; c) remove the child or remove other children from the vicinity; d) obtain extra help from other staff; e) some other response. Please describe. How effective are these strategies?

2. What do other staff present, e.g. classroom assistant, do when child behaves in
the what you have described?

3. Do you think that the management of
child's behaviour is your responsibility? If
no, who do you think is/should be responsible?

4. Does your child's behaviour involve you
in tasks or make demands on you which
you feel do not fall within the "normal"
role of the teacher (e.g. restraint, cleaning
up afterwards?)

5. What are your feelings towards N
when he/she has been behaving like this?

6. How do you deal with these feelings? Is
there anyone in the school whom you are
able to talk to?

7. Do you think that special skills are
needed for the management of child's
behaviour? If yes, please describe them.

8. What interventions have you tried with the child in the past? How successful were these?

9. Is there anything you would have liked to try but didn't? Why? Lack of time? Lack of skills? Lack of co-operation from other staff? Difficulties in organising?

10. What do you feel you can do now to help child?

11. What do you think is likely to happen to child during his/her time at school?

12. What do you think is likely to happen to child after he/she leaves school?

3. Procedures within the school in response to episodes of difficult behaviour

1. Who do you think should be responsible for difficult pupils? What should this responsibility entail?

2. When child behaves in the way you have described, do you report the incident to the headteacher or other members of staff? How do you do this?

3. Do you keep a record of incidents of challenging behaviour? How? Is this method of record keeping used throughout the school? Where is this record kept? Who has access to these records?

4. Do you carry out any written assessment of the child's behaviour? How? Has anyone else carried out a formal assessment? Who has access to the results of this assessment?

5. How do you decide on the best ways of working with the child?

6. Are other staff informed about the strategies that are being tried with a child? How is this done?

7. Does the school provide any support for staff who work with children with difficult behaviour?
Describe the support you get.

8. Do you refer to any other agencies or professionals for help in dealing with a child's behaviour? Who? How do you make the referral?

4. Relationships with parents

1. Do you ever give advice to N's parents on methods of working with him/her?

2. Do N's parents ever seek your advice about managing their child out of school?

3. Do you inform parents if you are going to carry out an assessment or implement a new strategy with N? How do you do this?

4. Are parents of N involved in working with children in your class? Are other parents involved in working in your class?

5. Are parents of N involved in the school in other ways? Are other parents involved in the school?

6. Are the family to your knowledge receiving any other form of support or help in managing the child's difficult behaviour e.g. visiting a Child Development Centre, or being seen by a hospital consultant?

5. Personal factors (answered at staff members' discretion)

1. What age group do you come in?
21-30, 30-40, 40-50, over 50.

2. a) Marital status
   b) Number of children

3. How long have you worked with:
a) Severe learning difficulties;
b) this school?

4. What area of teaching were you originally trained to teach?

5. Have you had any training in;

a) teaching special needs;

b) Severe learning difficulties;

c) dealing with challenging behaviours?

Please specify the training you have received.

6. Why do you work:

a) in the area of severe learning difficulties,

b) with children with challenging behaviour?

7. Do you think that children with severe learning difficulties should be integrated with other children or taught in segregated situations?
Please give reasons for your answer.

8. What are your present concerns about the education of these pupils?

9. Do you think that the teaching of pupils with severe learning difficulties and challenging behaviour requires:

a) special skills,

b) special personal qualities?

What are these special skills and/or qualities? Why do you think they are necessary?

10. How do you think teachers of pupils with severe learning difficulties and challenging behaviour are perceived by:

a) other special needs teachers;

b) other teachers;

c) the general public?

11. Do you intend to continue your teaching career in this field of work? If no, what work would you like to do?

BEHAVIOUR RECORDING SHEETS

* This pack contains five sheets for recording the child's behaviour during one day.

* Each sheet refers to one period of time, i.e. before morning break, after morning break, lunchtime, before afternoon break, and late afternoon.

* You have five packs; we would like you to make a record of the pupils behaviour for FIVE DAYS over a period of two weeks.

* Complete all sections for the five periods in each day, even when no difficult behaviour has occurred.

* Please describe the child's behaviour in terms of what the child actually did; avoid "fuzzy" descriptions e.g. "John hit Andrew on the head with the bat", rather than "John was aggressive", or "John tried to open the door, but couldn't; he then kicked the door", rather than "John was frustrated".

* Again, under "staff response", please describe what staff actually did at the time.

* Under "outcome", describe what happened for the child, the other children and/or the staff as appropriate.

BEHAVIOUR RECORDING - STAFF RESPONSE SHEET

Recording carried out by:

Date:

Time	Situation/ Context/ Activity	Adults/ pupils present	Pupil's behaviour - for incidents, comment on their nature; for other times, comment on pupil's involvement in activities.	Staff response - for incidents, what did staff member do; for other times, response to pupil's involvement.	Outcome / what happened next

Comments / Discussion:

Action:

SELF-REPORT QUESTIONNAIRE FOR STAFF WORKING WITH PUPILS WITH CHALLENGING BEHAVIOURS

The information you provide when completing this questionnaire will provide you and other members of staff with an overview of the challenges presented by this child. Be as accurate as possible in describing the pupil as he or she is NOW.

1. Name of pupil (N): ....

   Age: ....

2. Class: ....

   Teacher: ....

3. Person completing questionnaire
   if different from above. ....

   ....

   ....

A CLOSER LOOK AT PROBLEM BEHAVIOURS

4. Describe the things N does
   which create problems:

   Behaviour 1: ....

   ....

   Behaviour 2: ....

   ....

   Behaviour 3: ....

   ....

   Behaviour 4: ....

   ....

   Behaviour 5: ....

   ....

Before you go on stop and check you have described BEHAVIOURS. To do this, imagine one of your colleagues reads your description and asks "What do you mean?" Can you DEMONSTRATE the behaviour you have described? If you can it is probably a good description; if not, try again.

5. For each challenging behaviour provide the following information:

(a) How often do the behaviours occur? *Circle as appropriate.*

At least:

Behaviour 1:	*once per hour*	*once per day*	*once per week*
Behaviour 2:	*once per hour*	*once per day*	*once per week*
Behaviour 3:	*once per hour*	*once per day*	*once per week*
Behaviour 4:	*once per hour*	*once per day*	*once per week*
Behaviour 5:	*once per hour*	*once per day*	*once per week*

(b) How disruptive is the behaviour? Use the following scale to rate each behaviour you have described.

1 = little disruption to class activities

2 = temporary disruption for some pupils

3 = temporary disruption for most of class

4 = disruption for more than a few minutes

5 = behaviour requires intervention of other staff and/or removal of N or other pupils

Disruption Rating

Behaviour 1:	1	2	3	4	5
Behaviour 2:	1	2	3	4	5
Behaviour 3:	1	2	3	4	5
Behaviour 4:	1	2	3	4	5
Behaviour 5:	1	2	3	4	5

(c) What is the likelihood of personal injury to the child or others as a result of this behaviour? Use the following scale to rate each behaviour you have described.

1 = no risk of injury to N or others

2 = risk of <u>minor</u> injury to N or others

3 = <u>minor</u> injury to N or others <u>occurs or is likely to occur</u>

4 = risk of <u>serious</u> injury to N or others

5 = <u>serious</u> injury to N or others <u>occurs or is likely to occur</u>

<u>Danger Rating</u>

Behaviour 1:   1 2 3 4 5

Behaviour 2:   1 2 3 4 5

Behaviour 3:   1 2 3 4 5

Behaviour 4:   1 2 3 4 5

Behaviour 5:   1 2 3 4 5

6. On the basis of frequency, disruption and danger, select N's three most challenging behaviours.

Most challenging behaviour: ....

Second most challenging behaviour: ....

Third most challenging behaviour: ....

7. How do these behaviours create problems for N?

(i) Isolation from peers ....

(ii) Lack of access to the curriculum ....

(iii) Lack of access to extra curricular activities ....

(iv) Physical injury or risk of injury ....

(v) Other (describe) ....

....

8. How does N's behaviour create problems for other children?

    (i)   Disruption of teaching and
           learning ....

    (ii)   Disruption of play and leisure ....

    (iii) Injury or risk of injury ....

    (iv)   Other (describe) ....

9. Is there any pattern to the child's
    challenging behaviour   YES   NO

    Do they tend to occur:

    (i)   In certain situations - describe: ....

           ....

    (ii)   At particular times of the
           day - describe: ....

           ....

    (iii) In some places rather
           than others - describe: ....

           ....

    (iv)   When N is with special
           people - describe: ....

           ....

    (v)   Other - describe: ....

           ....

10. Are you able to predict when a
    problem is going to arise?   YES   NO

    If YES describe what you look for ....

    ....

11. As far as you know, is N taking
    any drugs or medication at the
    moment?   YES   NO

    If YES:
    (i)   What are the drugs?   ....

    (ii)   Do you feel they help N?   ....

    (iii)   How often are they taken?   ....

    (iv)   Are you aware of any side effects? ....

STAFF RESPONSES TO N's CHALLENGING BEHAVIOURS

12. What do you do when N behaves in the way you have described?

    (i)   Ignore N and to avoid the
            problem   ....

    (ii)   Attempt to divert or distract   ....

    (iii)   Remove N   ....

    (iv)   Remove other pupils   ....

    (v)   Get help from other staff   ....

    (vi)   Other - describe   ....

    Which of the above strategies do you feel is effective? Indicate by writing E
    (effective) against those strategies which USUALLY work.

13. What do other staff who work with N do when confronted by the behaviours you
    have described?

    (i)   Ignore N and try to avoid
            the problem.   ....

    (ii)   Attempt to divert or distract   ....

    (iii)   Remove N   ....

    (iv)   Remove other pupils   ....

    (v)   Get help from other staff   ....

    (vi)   Other - describe   ....

Are there any differences between your responses to questions 12 and 13?

14. Who do you think is currently responsible for dealing with N when he or she behaves in the way you have described?

    (i)   You

    (ii)   One of your classroom support workers

    (iii)   Another teacher

    (iv)   The headteacher

15. How do you feel when N is behaving like this?

    (i)   Angry

    (ii)   Upset

    (iii)   Stressed

    (iv)   Anxious

    (v)   Afraid

    (vi)   Frustrated

    (vii) Determined

    (viii) Other - describe

16. How do you deal with these feelings?

    (i)   Talk to other members of staff

    (ii)   Become bad tempered

    (iii)   Bottle it up till later

    (iv)   Try not to think about your feelings

    (v)   Other - describe

WHOLE SCHOOL INVOLVEMENT

17. When N behaves in the way you have described, do you report the incident to your headteacher?   YES   NO

18. Do you keep a record of when these behaviours occur?   YES   NO

    If YES, is this method of record keeping established throughout the school?   YES   NO

    Are the records used to try and understand why pupils present challenging behaviours?   YES   NO

19. Have you or anyone else carried out
a formal assessment of N's behaviour
in the last three months?   YES   NO

     If YES, what were the results..

20. Are other staff informed about
strategies being used to help
overcome the behaviours you
have described?   YES   NO

     If YES, how is this done?

21. Does the school provide support
especially for staff who work with
pupils who present challenging
behaviours?   YES   NO

     If Yes, what support do you receive?

INVOLVEMENT OF PARENTS AND OTHER AGENCIES

22. To your knowledge, are any other agencies involved in working to overcome the
behaviours you have described?

    (i)   Social Services

    (ii)   School medical officer

    (iii)   Family doctor

    (iv)   Educational psychologist

    (v)   Physiotherapist

    (vi)   Occupational therapist

    (vii)   Speech therapist

    (viii)   Other - describe

23. Who is responsible for liaising with
the other agencies who are working
with N

24. Do you generally keep N's parents
    (or carers) informed about the
    behaviours you have described?   YES   NO

    If YES, how do you do this:

    (i)   letters home

    (ii)   home school diary

    (iii)   telephone calls

    (iv)   visits by parents (or
           carers) to school

    (v)   visits by you to N's home

25. Do N's parents ever seek your
    advise on how to manage N's
    behaviour?   YES   NO

26. Do you ever offer advice to N's
    parents about how they might
    help overcome the behaviours
    you have described   YES   NO

THE NEXT STEP

Using this information, you should now be able to write a brief report covering the following areas:

What challenging behaviours should be addressed first and why?

Is there any pattern to N's challenging behaviours? Is medication a factor?

Current way of responding to N's challenging behaviours - is it consistent and is it effective? Comment on your strengths and weaknesses and areas where you feel you need more support/information/training. Be honest about your own feelings.

Challenging behaviour is an issue for the whole school; to what extent are other staff in your school involved? How could this be improved?

Are N's parents kept informed about what the school is doing? If other agencies are involved, who is responsible for co-ordinating various forms of help?

Remember, at this stage, you are not looking for solutions; instead you are trying to be clear about what behaviours are causing concern and the framework for special help which already exists.

EVALUATION OF INTERVENTION IN SCHOOLS (CLASSROOM TEACHERS) QUESTIONNAIRE

Name of School: .... Date ....

The following questions are designed to help us establish the effectiveness of our work in schools. All the items should be answered in respect of the changes which have been introduced as a direct result of your involvement with the project. We do not need your name. All responses will be treated in strictest confidence.

For multiple choice questions please circle your answer e.g. *not sure*

SECTION ONE: Your satisfaction with the organisation and outcomes of the project

Organisation of the project

1. How satisfied are you with the **whole school meetings** at the start of the project

    Very satisfied   *Not sure*   *Dissatisfied*   *Very dissatisfied*

    If dissatisfied or very dissatisfied please state reasons

    ....

    ....

2. How satisfied are you with the way in which **pupils were selected** for involvement in the project?

    Very satisfied   *Not sure*   *Dissatisfied*   *Very dissatisfied*

    If dissatisfied or very dissatisfied please state reasons

    ....

    ....

3. How satisfied are you with the **self report questionnaire** we used to collect information about pupils with challenging behaviours?

    Very satisfied   *Not sure*   *Dissatisfied*   *Very dissatisfied*

    If dissatisfied or very dissatisfied please state reasons

    ....

    ....

4. How satisfied are you with the way in which **'shadowing'** was carried out?

Very satisfied   *Not sure*   *Dissatisfied*   *Very dissatisfied*

If dissatisfied or very dissatisfied please state reasons

....

....

5(a) How satisfied are you with the training you received from Margaret Cook on observing and recording pupils' behaviour?

Very satisfied   *Not sure*   *Dissatisfied*   *Very dissatisfied*

If dissatisfied or very dissatisfied please state reasons

....

....

5(b) How satisfied are you with **your involvement in recording pupils' behaviour?**

Very satisfied   *Not sure*   *Dissatisfied*   *Very dissatisfied*

If dissatisfied or very dissatisfied please state reasons

....

....

6. How satisfied are you with the way in which the **review meetings** were carried out?

Very satisfied   *Not sure*   *Dissatisfied*   *Very dissatisfied*

If dissatisfied or very dissatisfied please state reasons

....

....

7. How satisfied are you with the **outcome of the review meetings?**

Very satisfied   *Not sure*   *Dissatisfied*   *Very dissatisfied*

If dissatisfied or very dissatisfied please state reasons

....

....

8. How satisfied are you with the **intervention programme** which was agreed at the review meeting?

   Very satisfied   *Not sure*   *Dissatisfied*   *Very dissatisfied*

   If dissatisfied or very dissatisfied please state reasons

   ....

   ....

9. How satisfied are you with the **support you received from the project** team while you carrying out the intervention programme?

   Very satisfied   *Not sure*   *Dissatisfied*   *Very dissatisfied*

   If dissatisfied or very dissatisfied please state reasons

   ....

   ....

10. How satisfied are you with the **support you received from your headteacher** during the project?

    Very satisfied   *Not sure*   *Dissatisfied*   *Very dissatisfied*

    If dissatisfied or very dissatisfied please state reasons

    ....

    ....

11. How satisfied are you with the **involvement of other members of the teaching staff** in the project?

    Very satisfied   *Not sure*   *Dissatisfied*   *Very dissatisfied*

    If dissatisfied or very dissatisfied please state reasons

    ....

    ....

12. How satisfied are you with the **involvement of the classroom support workers** in the project?

    Very satisfied   *Not sure*   *Dissatisfied*   *very dissatisfied*

    If dissatisfied or very dissatisfied please state reasons

    ....

    ....

13. How satisfied are you with the **involvement of parents** in the project?

    Very satisfied   *Not sure*   *Dissatisfied*   *Very dissatisfied*

    If dissatisfied or very dissatisfied please state reasons

    ....

    ....

14. How satisfied are you that the project **resulted in positive outcomes for the selected pupil(s)** in your class?

    Very satisfied   *Not sure*   *Dissatisfied*   *Very dissatisfied*

    If dissatisfied or very dissatisfied please state reasons

    ....

    ....

15. How satisfied are you that the project resulted in **positive outcomes for the other pupils** in your class who were not directly involved?

    Very satisfied   *Not sure*   *Dissatisfied*   *Very dissatisfied*

    If dissatisfied or very dissatisfied please state reasons

    ....

    ....

16. How satisfied are you that the project resulted in **positive outcomes for the school as a whole?**

    Very satisfied   *Not sure*   *Dissatisfied*   *Very dissatisfied*

    If dissatisfied or very dissatisfied please state reasons

    ....

    ....

END OF SECTION ONE

(You may need a break before you go on!)

SECTION TWO: How effective was the project?

The following questions refer to procedures you carried out as a direct result of your involvement with the project. Please answer one set of questions for each pupil in your class who was selected for intervention.

This is for pupil No. 1 2 3 (please circle one number).

For multiple choice questions please circle your answer e.g. (Yes) No where your answer is *Yes*

1. Have you changed the way in which you respond to incidents of challenging behaviour as a result of your involvement with the project?

   Yes   No

   If *Yes* is the new approach:

   (a) more effective than those used in the past

   (b) less effective than those used in the past

   (c) neither more nor less effective than other approaches already tried

   (please circle)

2. Have you introduced any new strategies for **preventing or decreasing the occurrence** of challenging behaviours?

   Yes   No

   If *Yes* have these strategies produced any changes in the pupils behaviour?

   (a) increase in occurrence of challenging behaviours

   (b) no change in occurrence of challenging behaviours

   (c) less frequent incidents of challenging behaviours

   (d) incidents of challenging behaviour are less intense

   (e) challenging behaviours last for a shorter period of time

   (f) other 'new' challenging behaviours have appeared

   (please circle)

3. Are you aware of any changes in the occurrence of challenging behaviours **when this pupil is with other members of staff?**

    (a)   increase in occurrence of challenging behaviours

    (b)   no change in occurrence of challenging behaviours

    (c)   less frequent incidents of challenging behaviours

    (d)   incidents of challenging behaviour are less intense

    (e)   challenging behaviours last for a shorter period of time

    (f)   other 'new' challenging behaviours have appeared

    (please circle)

4. As a result of your involvement in the project, have you done anything different to **help this pupil learn new skills?**

    Yes   *No*

    If *Yes* how successful have your efforts to teach new skills been?

    (a)   not successful

    (b)   somewhat successful - unsure

    (c)   very successful - clear evidence of new skills

    (please circle)

5. If you feel you have been successful in teaching new skills, have these **new skills made any difference to your management of the child's challenging behaviours?**

    Yes   *No*

    If *Yes* please describe briefly:

    ....

    ....

6. As a result of your involvement in the project, has there been any change in the extent to which this **pupil participates in group activities?**

    (a)   no change in participation in group activities

    (b)   participates less in group activities

    (c)   participates in more group activities

    (please circle)

7. As a result of your involvement in the project, has there been any change in the way in which **other pupils interact with this pupil?**

   (a)   increase in positive social interactions

   (b)   increase in negative/hostile social interactions

   (c)   reduction in positive social interactions

   (d)   reduction in negative/hostile social interactions

   (e)   no change

   (please circle)

8. As a result of your involvement in this project, has there been any change in the way in which **you are able to interact with this pupil?**

   (a)   increase in positive social interactions

   (b)   increase in negative/hostile social interactions

   (c)   reduction in positive social interactions

   (d)   reduction in negative/hostile social interactions

   (e)   no change

   (please circle)

9. As a result of this pupil's involvement in the project, have there been any changes in the way in which the **pupil interacts with classroom support workers?**

   (a)   increase in positive social interactions

   (b)   increase in negative/hostile social interactions

   (c)   reduction in positive social interactions

   (d)   reduction in negative/hostile social interactions

   (e)   no change

   (please circle)

SECTION THREE: Development of expertise by staff

Please answer these questions in relation to your involvement in the project. Please try to distinguish **what you did as part of the project** and what you feel **able to do now as a result of the project.**

For multiple choice questions please circle your answer e.g. (Yes) No where your answer is *Yes*.

A.   Identification of challenging behaviours

1.   What do you understand by the term *challenging behaviour?*

....

....

2.   Have your views on challenging behaviours changed as a result of your involvement in the project?

       Yes   *No*   *Not sure*

If *Yes* please describe the changes.

....

....

3.   Did the project help you to identify challenging behaviours?

       Yes   *No*   *Not sure*

4.   **Following your involvement** with the project, are you confident that you can identify challenging behaviours when they occur in other children?

       Yes   *No*   *Not sure*

If *Yes* have you done this since the project finished?

B.   RECORDING CHALLENGING BEHAVIOURS

5.   **During the project** were you able to make an <u>accurate record</u> of incidents of challenging behaviours?

       Yes   *No*   *Not sure*

If *No* please state reasons:

....

....

6. **Following your involvement** in the project, how confident are you that you could <u>make your own record of incidents</u> of challenging behaviours presented by other pupils?

Very confident   *Quite confident*   *Not sure*   *Not at all confident*

If *not sure* or *Not at all confident* please state reasons:

If *Very confident* or *Quite confident* have you done this since the project finished?

Yes   *No*

C. **Strategies for responding to incidents of challenging behaviours**

7. **During the project**, were you able to <u>agree on strategies</u> for responding to incidents of challenging behaviours?

Yes   *No*   *Not sure*

If *No* please state reasons:

8. **Following your involvement** with the project, how confident are you that you could <u>work out your own strategy</u> for responding to incidents of challenging behaviour?

Very confident   *Quite confident*   *Not sure*   *Not at all confident*

If *Not sure* or *Not at all confident* please state reasons:

If *very confident* or *Quite confident* have you done this since the project finished?

Yes   *No*

9. **During the project** were you able to <u>implement strategies</u> for responding to incidents of challenging behaviours?

Yes   *No*   *Not sure*

If *No* please state reasons:

10. **Following the project**, how confident are you that you could implement your own strategies for responding to incidents of challenging behaviours?

    Very confident   *Quite confident*   *Not sure*   *Not at all confident*

    If *Not sure* or *Not at all confident* please state reasons

    ....

    ....

    If *Very confident* or *Quite confident* have you done this since the project finished?

    Yes   *No*

D.   Strategies for reducing occurrence of challenging behaviour

11. **During the project** were you able to agree on a strategy for reducing the occurrence of challenging behaviours?

    Yes   *No*   *Not sure*

    If *No* please state reasons:

    ....

    ....

12. **Following the project** how confident are you that you could develop a new strategy for reducing the occurrence of challenging behaviour in another pupil?

    Very confident   *Quite confident*   *Not sure*   *Not at all confident*

    If *Not sure* or *Not at all confident* please state reasons?

    ....

    ....

    If *Very confident* or *Quite confident* have you done this since the project finished?

    Yes   *No*

13. **During the project** were you able to implement a strategy for reducing the occurrence of challenging behaviours in another pupil?

    Yes   *No*   *Not sure*

    If *No* please state reasons

    ....

    ....

14. **Following the project** how confident are you that you could <u>implement a strategy</u> for reducing the occurrence of challenging behaviour in another pupil?

   Very confident   *Quite confident*   *Not sure*   *Not at all confident*

   If *Not sure* or *Not at all confident* please state reasons:

   ....

   ....

   If *Very confident* or *Quite confident* have you done this since the project finished?

   Yes   *No*

E.   Strategies for teaching new skills to pupils with challenging behaviours

15. **During the project** were you able to agree a <u>strategy for teaching new skills</u> to the selected pupil(s)?

   Yes   *No*   *Not sure*

   If *No* please state reasons:

   ....

   ....

16. **Following the project** how confident are you that you could <u>develop your own strategy</u> for helping a pupil with challenging behaviours to learn new skills?

   Very confident   *Quite confident*   *Not sure*   *Not at all confident*

   If *Not sure* or *Not at all confident* please state reasons:

   ....

   ....

   If *Very confident* or *Quite confident* have you done this since the project finished?

   Yes   *No*

17. **During the project** were you able to <u>implement a strategy</u> for teaching new skills to a pupil with challenging behaviours?

   Yes   *No*   *Not sure*

   If *No* please state reasons

   ....

   ....

18. **Following the project** how confident are you that you could <u>implement your own strategy</u> for teaching new skills to another pupil with challenging behaviours?

    Very confident   *Quite confident*   *Not sure*   *Not at all confident*

    If *Not sure* or *Not at all confident* please state reasons:

    ....

    ....

    If *Very confident* or *Quite confident* have you done this since the project finished?

        Yes   *No*

F.   **Strategies for involving pupils with challenging behaviours in group work**

19. **During the project** were you able to <u>agree a strategy</u> for involving a child with challenging behaviours in group activities?

        Yes   *No*   *Not sure*

    If *No* please state reasons:

    ....

20. **Following the project** how confident are you that you could <u>develop your own strategies</u> for involving a child with challenging behaviours in group activities?

    Very confident   *Quite confident*   *Not sure*   *Not at all confident*

    If *Not sure* or *Not at all confident* please state reasons:

    ....

    If *Very confident* or *Quite confident* please state reasons:

    ....

    If *Very confident* or *Quite confident* have you done this since the project finished?

        Yes   *No*

21. **During the project** were you able to <u>implement a strategy</u> for involving a child with challenging behaviours in group activities?

        Yes   *No*   *Not sure*

    If *No* please state reasons

    ....

    ....

22. **Following the project** how confident are you that you could <u>implement your own strategy</u> for involving a child with challenging behaviours in group activities?

Very confident   *Quite confident*   *Not sure*   *Not at all confident*

If *Not sure* or *Not at all confident* please state reasons:

....

....

If *Very confident* or *Quite confident* have you done this since the project finished?

    Yes   *No*

G. Working together with classroom support workers

23. **During the project** were you able to work successfully with your classroom support worker in the following areas:

    (a)   identifying target pupils   *Yes*   *No*

    (b)   identifying challenging behaviours   *Yes*   *No*

    (c)   recording incidents of challenging behaviours   *Yes*   *No*

    (d)   developing strategies for intervention   *Yes*   *No*

    (e)   implementing strategies   *Yes*   *No*

24. **Following the project** are you confident that you can continue to work with your classroom support worker in the following areas:

    (a)   identifying target pupils   *Yes*   *No*

    (b)   identifying challenging behaviours   *Yes*   *No*

    (c)   recording incidents of challenging behaviours   *Yes*   *No*

    (d)   developing strategies for intervention   *Yes*   *No*

    (e)   implementing strategies   *Yes*   *No*

H. Working together with other teachers

25. **During the project** were you able to work successfully with other teachers in the following areas:

    (a)   identifying target pupils   *Yes*   *No*

    (b)   identifying challenging behaviours   *Yes*   *No*

(c)   recording incidents of challenging behaviours   *Yes*   *No*

(d)   developing strategies for intervention   *Yes*   *No*

(e)   implementing strategies   *Yes*   *No*

26. **Following the project** are you confident that you can continue to work successfully with other teachers in the following areas:

    (a)   identifying target pupils   *Yes*   *No*

    (b)   identifying challenging behaviours   *Yes*   *No*

    (c)   recording incidents of challenging behaviours   *Yes*   *No*

    (d)   developing strategies for intervention   *Yes*   *No*

    (e)   implementing strategies   *Yes*   *No*

I.   A whole school strategy

27. **During the project** to what extent was a whole school strategy employed for helping the selected pupils in your class?

    (a)   successful whole school strategy

    (b)   moderately successful whole school strategy

    (c)   whole school strategy never properly introduced

    (tick one)

28. How confident are you that a whole school approach to helping pupils with challenging behaviours will be **maintained in the future?**

    Very confident   *Quite confident*   *Not very confident*

J.   Overall

29. What is the **single most important** outcome from your involvement in the project?

30. What still needs to be done in your school to ensure that pupils with challenging behaviours receive appropriate help?

31. Are there any other comments you wish to make?

....

....

....

....

....

END OF SECTION THREE (At last!)

Thank you for taking the trouble to complete this questionnaire

Please return it in the envelope provided to:

Margaret Cook
The University of Birmingham
Edgbaston
Birmingham. B15 2TT.

EVALUATION OF INTERVENTION IN SCHOOLS (Classroom Support Workers) QUESTIONNAIRE

Name of school: .... Date: ....

The following questions are designed to help us establish the effectiveness of our work in schools. All the items should be answered in respect of the changes which have been introduced as a direct result of your involvement with the project. We do not need your name. All responses will be treated in strictest confidence.

For multiple choice questions please circle your answer e.g. *not sure*

Organisation of the project

1. How satisfied are you with the **whole school meetings** at the start of the project?

    Very satisfied　　　*Not sure*　　　*Dissatisfied*　　　*Very dissatisfied*

    If dissatisfied or very dissatisfied please state reasons

    ....

    ....

2. How satisfied are you with the way in which **pupils were selected** for involvement in the project?

    Very satisfied　　　*Not sure*　　　*Dissatisfied*　　　*Very dissatisfied*

    If dissatisfied or very dissatisfied please state reasons

    ....

    ....

3. How satisfied are you with the way in which **'shadowing'** was carried out?

    Very satisfied　　　*Not sure*　　　*Dissatisfied*　　　*Very dissatisfied*

    If dissatisfied or very dissatisfied please state reasons

    ....

    ....

4. How satisfied are you with **your involvement in recording pupils' behaviour?**

    Very satisfied   *Not sure*   *Dissatisfied*   *Very dissatisfied*

    If dissatisfied or very dissatisfied please state reasons

    ....

    ....

5. How satisfied are you with the way in which the **review meetings** were carried out?

    Very satisfied   *Not sure*   *Dissatisfied*   *Very dissatisfied*

    If dissatisfied or very dissatisfied please state reasons

    ....

    ....

6. How satisfied are you with the **outcome of the review meetings?**

    Very satisfied   *Not sure*   *Dissatisfied*   *Very dissatisfied*

    If dissatisfied or very dissatisfied please state reasons

    ....

    ....

7. How satisfied are you with the **intervention programme** which was agreed at the review meeting?

    Very satisfied   *Not sure*   *Dissatisfied*   *Very dissatisfied*

    If dissatisfied or very dissatisfied please state reasons

    ....

    ....

8. How satisfied are you with the **support you received from the project team** while carrying out the intervention programme?

    Very satisfied   *Not sure*   *Dissatisfied*   *Very dissatisfied*

    If dissatisfied or very dissatisfied please state reasons

    ....

    ....

9. How satisfied are you with the **support you received from the teaching staff** in the project?

   Very satisfied   *Not sure*   *Dissatisfied*   *Very dissatisfied*

   If dissatisfied or very dissatisfied please state reasons

   ....

   ....

10. How satisfied are you with the **involvement of parents** in the project?

    Very satisfied   *Not sure*   *Dissatisfied*   *Very dissatisfied*

    If dissatisfied or very dissatisfied please state reasons

    ....

    ....

11. How satisfied are you that the project **resulted in positive outcomes for the selected pupil(s)** in your class?

    Very satisfied   *Not sure*   *Dissatisfied*   *Very dissatisfied*

    If dissatisfied or very dissatisfied please state reasons

    ....

    ....

12. How satisfied are you that the project resulted in **positive outcomes for the other pupils** in your class who were not directly involved?

    Very satisfied   *Not sure*   *Dissatisfied*   *Very dissatisfied*

    If dissatisfied or very dissatisfied please state reasons

    ....

    ....

13. How satisfied are you that the project resulted in **positive outcomes for the school as a whole**?

    Very satisfied   *Not sure*   *Dissatisfied*   *Very dissatisfied*

    If dissatisfied or very dissatisfied please state reasons

    ....

    ....

14. What is the **single most important outcome** from your involvement in the project?

15. **What still needs to be done** in your class to ensure that pupils with challenging behaviours receive appropriate help?

16. Any other comments you wish to make:

Thank you for taking the trouble to complete this questionnaire.

Please return it in the envelope provided to:

Margaret Cook,
The University of Birmingham,
Edgbaston,
Birmingham, B15 2TT.

EVALUATION OF INTERVENTION IN SCHOOLS (Headteachers) QUESTIONNAIRE

Name of school: .... Date: ....

The following questions are designed to help us establish the effectiveness of our work in schools. All the items should be answered in respect of the changes which have been introduced as a direct result of your involvement with the project. We do not need your name. All responses will be treated in strictest confidence.

For multiple choice questions please circle your answer e.g. *not sure*

Organisation of the project

1. How satisfied are you with the **whole school meetings** at the start of the project?

    Very satisfied   *Not sure*   *Dissatisfied*   *Very dissatisfied*

    If dissatisfied or very dissatisfied please state reasons

    ....

    ....

2. How satisfied are you with the way in which **pupils were selected** for involvement in the project?

    Very satisfied   *Not sure*   *Dissatisfied*   *Very dissatisfied*

    If dissatisfied or very dissatisfied please state reasons

    ....

    ....

3. How satisfied are you with the way in which **'shadowing'** was carried out?

    Very satisfied   *Not sure*   *Dissatisfied*   *Very dissatisfied*

    If dissatisfied or very dissatisfied please state reasons

    ....

    ....

4. How satisfied are you with **your involvement in recording pupils' behaviour?**

    Very satisfied   *Not sure*   *Dissatisfied*   *Very dissatisfied*

    If dissatisfied or very dissatisfied please state reasons

    ....

    ....

5. How satisfied are you with the way in which the **review meetings** were carried out?

    Very satisfied   *Not sure*   *Dissatisfied*   *Very dissatisfied*

    If dissatisfied or very dissatisfied please state reasons

    ....

    ....

6. How satisfied are you with the **outcome of the review meetings?**

    Very satisfied   *Not sure*   *Dissatisfied*   *Very dissatisfied*

    If dissatisfied or very dissatisfied please state reasons

    ....

    ....

7. How satisfied are you with the **intervention programme** which was agreed at the review meeting?

    Very satisfied   *Not sure*   *Dissatisfied*   *Very dissatisfied*

    If dissatisfied or very dissatisfied please state reasons

    ....

    ....

8. How satisfied are you with the **support you received from the project team** while carrying out the intervention programme?

    Very satisfied   *Not sure*   *Dissatisfied*   *Very dissatisfied*

    If dissatisfied or very dissatisfied please state reasons

    ....

    ....

9. How satisfied are you with the **involvement of members of the teaching staff** in the project?

Very satisfied   *Not sure*   *Dissatisfied*   *Very dissatisfied*

If dissatisfied or very dissatisfied please state reasons

10. How satisfied are you with the **involvement of the classroom support workers** in the project?

Very satisfied   *Not sure*   *Dissatisfied*   *Very satisfied*

If dissatisfied or very dissatisfied please state reasons

11. How satisfied are you with the **involvement of parents** in the project?

Very satisfied   *Not sure*   *Dissatisfied*   *Very dissatisfied*

If dissatisfied or very dissatisfied please state reasons

12. How satisfied are you that the project **resulted in positive outcomes for the selected pupil(s)** in your school?

Very satisfied   *Not sure*   *Dissatisfied*   *Very dissatisfied*

If dissatisfied or very dissatisfied please state reasons

13. How satisfied are you that the project resulted in **positive outcomes for the other pupils** in your school who were not directly involved?

very satisfied   *Not sure*   *Dissatisfied*   *Very dissatisfied*

If dissatisfied or very dissatisfied please state reasons

14. How satisfied are you that the project resulted in **positive outcomes for the school as a whole?**

    Very satisfied   *Not sure*   *Dissatisfied*   *Very dissatisfied*

    If dissatisfied or very dissatisfied please state reasons

    ....

    ....

15. During the project, to what extent was a **whole school strategy** employed for helping the selected pupils?

    (a)   successful whole school strategy

    (b)   moderately successful whole school strategy

    (c)   Whole school strategy never properly introduced

    (please circle)

16. How confident are you that a whole school approach to helping pupils with challenging behaviours **will be maintained in the future?**

    Very confident   *Quite confident*   *Not very confident*

17. What is the **single most important outcome** from your involvement in the project?

    ....

    ....

    ....

    ....

18. **What still needs to be done** in your school to ensure that pupils with challenging behaviours receive appropriate help?

    ....

    ....

    ....

    ....

    ....

    ....

19. Any other comments you wish to make:

....

....

....

....

....

Thank you for taking the trouble to complete this questionnaire.

Please return it in the envelope provided to:

Margaret Cook,
The University of Birmingham,
Edgbaston,
Birmingham, B15 2TT.

APPENDIX TWO

CONTENTS

Dates of teacher recording and observation by project staff

Appendix 2

Dates of teacher recording and observation by project staff

	Observation by Project Staff		Teacher recording			
	Pre	Post	Pre		Post	
			First	Last	First	Last
<u>Phase 1</u> **School/Pupil**						
Merry						
Alan	6,11,21 May	17 November				
Bright						
Colin	3, 5, 14 May	2 November				
Harry	5 May/ 3, 11 June	5 November				
Carol	3, 11 June	2 November/ 1 December				
Pleasant						
Nigel	13, 18 May					
John	29 April/ 10 June	12 November				
Friendly						
Charles	20 May					
Cliff	4 June	10 November				
Mary	20 May	23 November				
Happy						
Ben	9, 12 May					
Angela	1 June					
Stephen	May/1 June					

Appendix 2 (continued)

Dates of teacher recording and observation by project staff

| | Observation by Project Staff | | Teacher recording | | | |
| | Pre | Post | Pre | | Post | |
			First	Last	First	Last
Phase II						
School/Pupil						
Lively						
Jack	12,20 January	19 May	8 Jan 12 Jan	22 Jan	19 May	7 Jul
Neil	30 November	24 May	14 Dec	22 Jan	17 May	14 Jun
Mick	3 December/ 20 January	2 June		3 Jan	9 Jun	18 Jun
Jolly						
Ruth	14 jan	18 May	5 Jan	14 Jan	17 Jun	25 Jun
Adam	10 December	18 May	8 Dec	15 Jan	10 May	21 May
Darren	21 January	26 May	9 Dec	20 Jan	10 May	20 May
Joyful						
Martin	16, 24 Nov/ 9 December	17 May	1 Dec	10 Dec	1 May	19 May
Michael	16, 23 Nov 9 December	27 May	8 Dec	20 Jan		
Simon	16 November 7 December		30 Nov	7 Dec	13 May	19 May
Cheerful						
Clive	1, 5 February		3 Mar	12 mar	21 Jun	29 Jun
Chris	11, 24 February	10, 22 June	25 Feb	17 Mar	30 Jun	8 Jul

Subject Index

Name Index